Connect With Ruthless Honesty

CONNECT WITH
RUTHLESS
HONESTY

The Freedom to Succeed in Life and in Business

PETE DE LA TORRE
First Edition

CONNECT WITH RUTHLESS HONESTY

The Freedom to Succeed in Life and in Business

© 2023 Pete De La Torre

All rights reserved.

No part of this book may be reproduced or transmitted in any form without written permission from the publisher or author, except as permitted by U.S. copyright law.

This publication is designed to provide accurate and authoritative information in regard to the subject matter covered. It is sold with the understanding that neither the author nor the publisher is engaged in rendering legal or other professional services. While the publisher and author have used their best efforts in preparing this book, the purpose of this book is to educate and give suggestions. The authors and publisher shall have neither liability nor responsibility to any person or entity with respect to any loss or damage caused or alleged to have been caused directly or indirectly by the information contained in this book.

Printed in the United States of America

First Edition

ISBN 979-8-218-18682-1 paperback
ISBN 979-8-218-18681-4 ebook
Library of Congress Control Number: 2023906342

Cover and Interior Design by:
Chris Treccani

DEDICATION

To my beautiful parents—Lucas and Rosario—the two most loving and caring people I have ever known:
Even though we lost both of you twelve days apart in 2008, your influence, example of goodness, and love for God resonate with me more than ever. You were deeply loved and respected by everyone who was privileged to know you. I miss you each and every day!

To my children—Melissa and Michael:
Words cannot express how grateful and humbled I am to be your dad. Your dedication, hard work, humor, and love for family is an inspiration to me every single day. Yet what I'm proudest of is your hearts of gold. I love you, Pop.

To my three amigos—my grandsons Andrew, Adrian, and Aiden: You have a shining and luminous future. Abuelo loves you!

To my brothers—Luke (RIP), Richie, and Phil:

We are the sons of Lucas and Rosario. I see Mom and Dad clearly in the three of you. Your genuine brotherly love touches me in ways I cannot describe. I love you guys!

To my stepsons and daughter—James, Julian, and Francesca:

Thank you for opening up your hearts to me. A special mention for little Santiago, the newest member of the family. I love you all.

Last but certainly not least, to my wife, Jacquelyn:

I still cannot believe we reunited after over 45 years. I am beyond grateful that God brought us together at this moment in our lives. Your tender, loving care and support overwhelms me. You are my life partner and biggest fan. I can't wait to experience the rest of our lives together. I love you very much!

CONTENTS

Foreword — ix
Introduction — xi

Part I: Life until 63 — 1
Chapter 1: Who I Was and Where I Came From — 3
Chapter 2: Wake-Up Call — 17

Part II: Marching Orders from God — 31
Chapter 3: My Self-Discovery — 33
Chapter 4: New Philosophy — 49

Part III: Walk the Talk — 67
Chapter 5: Wellness Trifecta — 69
Chapter 6: Business Transformation — 83

Part IV: The Road Ahead — 97
Chapter 7: Dig Deep, Rise Above, Reach Out, and Stay the Course — 99

Acknowledgments — 113
About the Author — 115
Resources — 117

FOREWORD

It was my pleasure to get to know Pete De La Torre during a conference where I gave a speech. Our encounter quickly became a friendship that has gone from mere acquaintance to a partnership for evangelizing how technology can decentralize prosperity. During the course of our friendship, I have watched Pete grow in his relationship with his faith and optimistic view on life, and I see how his heart burns with the desire to help others.

I have seen his career in broadcasting establish him as an honest, strong, and independent voice. I have deeply appreciated his family's contributions to the Miami region, to both English and Spanish speakers alike.

Every day, I see people doing great things in the world. What do they have in common? They display the same courage that Pete has, courage to go after their dreams and make a positive impact. Pete's faith has shown him that there are no limits to God. Anyone can have whatever they ask—if only they believe.

The only thing that limits what God can do in your life is your belief system. As you read this book, you will recognize that your life results are from what you've believed over the past weeks, months, and years. Therefore, to change your life, you must first improve your beliefs.

Pete discovered how to tap into the limitless grace and power of God by overcoming personal adversity, having faith, refusing to doubt, and believing the Word of God. He understood Yeshua's words, "Therefore I tell you, whatever you ask in prayer, believe that you have received it, and it will be yours." Pete applied this truth and has been able to think outside the box and believe in God for the impossible. The only requirement for his receiving was his belief.

In this priceless, thought-provoking, and timely book, Pete will share with you how to go deeper in gaining knowledge of the lifelong road we are all on. He will take you on a journey, sharing life experiences that will help you navigate your life and business based on dogged optimism, kindness, and genuine gratitude. I hope you enjoy getting to know Pete De La Torre as much as I have.

Sean Michael Brehm
Chairman & CEO CrowdPoint Technologies

INTRODUCTION

My life changed in the spring of 2021 when I heard the news that I had prostate cancer.

My battle with this horrible disease overwhelmed me with a predictable avalanche of emotions that was to be the catalyst for a dramatic personal transformation. What I learned in the process of fighting cancer revolutionized my life in ways I never could have imagined. I've been brutally reminded that I am a human being filled with flaws and imperfections.

As a result of this experience—and for the first time in my life—I am able to truly connect with myself and others in a way that is fulfilling beyond words. My eyes have opened to see the world in a way that I have never seen it before. I'm reminded of a phenomenal Beatles lyric, from the song "Strawberry Fields Forever," which says: "Living is easy with eyes closed, misunderstanding all you see!"

In many ways, I was blinded to reality for years. My interpretation of life was misguided. I was disconnected from the world and others. All that changed with my cancer diagnosis. I was reintroduced to life and the beauty of connecting with others. I felt a profound connection to the world that I couldn't explain. It was real and authentic.

This unexpected adversity was a game changer for me. I asked the big questions: "Why me?" and "Why now?"

I do know that there was a divine reason, a message from God that I should use this experience to help others going through the same ordeal, both from a medical and an emotional perspective. God pulled me through this and now he expects me to carry the torch, to speak on his behalf.

In writing this book, I faced the proverbial writer's block many times over. I just didn't have it; the ideas weren't coming, and I became more frustrated the harder I tried. That is when I did something that always works—I prayed for inspiration and direction, for the right words and the right flow. I surrendered the process and turned it over to God. After all, he was the one who inspired me to move forward with this book project. I was convinced that he was the spark I needed and that he would inspire me throughout the writing process, especially when I was stuck. I can confidently state that the words you are about to read are not my words but a message directly from the source, my loving God.

My purpose is to connect with you clearly and honestly through my words and experience, to share with you how my life has taken a completely different road than the one I was on. You will learn about my roller coaster ride through my cancer journey, how it dramatically shifted my focus to wellness, and how my business has been transformed. My appreciation for the power of connecting with the right people and the right solutions at the right time and for the right reasons is beyond description.

I will share my perspective on connecting, a perspective that I've gained over the years, especially through my encounter with cancer. I have learned that my success in life and in business is predicated on being the very best connector I can be, driven by integrity and authenticity.

By reading this book, you will be the beneficiary of all the knowledge and insights I've acquired over the years—including the many groundbreaking books I've read and studied, my professional experience over the last forty years, lessons learned from close family and friends, and priceless wisdom gained from many trusted mentors and advisors. I will also share million-dollar insights I've gained from my thirteen-plus years as an award-winning talk show host interviewing over 2,500 local and global influencers, executives, and community and government leaders.

As you read, you too will understand how important it is for you to be able to authentically connect your story with your family, friends, and the business world. To illustrate critical ideas, I will share scriptural wisdom directly from the King James Version (KJV) of the Bible and inspirational third-party quotes from some of the finest and best-known thought leaders. My hope is that you will embrace the concept of connecting the dots in all aspects of your life, making sure everything is aligning the way it is supposed to instead of forcing your way through life.

So, if you're ready, I humbly ask that you begin reading this book, for it is my divinely inspired gift for you so that you, too, will experience success and wellness in your life and business.

PART I

Life until 63

CHAPTER 1
Who I Was and Where I Came From

The following is my story, the story of a regular guy, the son of Cuban immigrants.

I had a life full of experiences, some good, some not so good. You will learn a little bit about me: Who I was, what I did and didn't do. How I reacted to the good and bad times. The choices I made or didn't make. How I was greatly affected by the teachings and examples of my parents and older siblings. The roller coaster of my personal journey of more than 63 years, from childhood to life as a father, grandfather, friend, and businessman. The hits and misses I endured, the disappointments and achievements. The regrets of falling short and of missed opportunities.

When you read through the story, you'll probably relate to my feelings and emotions. My story may inspire you or make you sad. You'll probably take time to contemplate your own story, what's happened to you and how it has affected you. You will realize that each of us has a story to tell—how we've lived and the challenges and adversity that have shifted our lives for better or worse.

You and I live a life that is full of ups and downs, successes and failures, joy and sadness. We have experiences reaching back to childhood that affect and influence us for the rest of our lives. We are molded by what we see and hear and the people that surround us.

In looking back, I concluded that I am a normal person—just like you—who has gone through life confronted by trials and tribulations. We are not immune to challenges. How we respond makes all the difference. Many times, we react rather than taking affirmative action. If we are not careful, negativity can push us in the wrong direction. It can hold us back from experiencing joy and being all that we can be. Every one of life's encounters is ingrained in our hearts and minds. As the years pass, so much of what happens to us is deposited in our subconscious. Slowly but surely, we develop a mindset and behavior pattern that is a byproduct of everything that's come our way and how we responded.

One influence on me was the fact that my parents moved twelve times from the time I was five until I was twenty, the year I got married. Every time I began to make friends, we moved to another neighborhood. We moved so many times, I wondered why we didn't start a moving company called De La Torre Moving. My older brother often joked that every time the full moon rose, my father would turn into a werewolf, get the itch, and decide to pack things up and move on to the next house.

Looking back, I realize that my parents were always running away rather than moving forward. I believe the reason my parents moved as often as they did was because of their limiting beliefs and lack of confidence that they could overcome their challenges. Their typical course of action was to move at the first sign of a setback.

Today, I know that my parents did the best they could. Their intentions were always to do what they believed was right. What they couldn't grasp is that the constant moving was scarring their sons by taking away much of their childhood. We never stayed in any home long enough to develop meaningful friends. We had many acquaintances but very few real friends.

Throughout our lives, we can either move too quickly, jumping the gun, or stay longer than we should. Moving too quickly is literally running away, while staying longer than you should is a sign of being afraid to make a decision that may be best for you. In either case, you probably have limiting beliefs and lack self-confidence.

As a child, I absorbed and internalized these traits, and they cursed and incarcerated me for most of my life, even though I didn't realize what was happening to me. True freedom was both foreign and fleeting for me. I never understood what it meant to truly live free. My mindset and my choices kept me in chains. My self-imposed isolation deceived me into thinking that I was protecting my turf. What was really happening? I was growing more disconnected from the real world and others. The disconnect I had from reality was alarming. Many times, my view on life was distorted and misguided.

Are you dealing with a trauma you suffered as a young child that is haunting you today, an experience that has left an ongoing and lingering effect on you? Perhaps a mysterious and unseen obstacle has routed your life down an unwanted path. If so, you and I have something in common.

The experience of my parents moving so frequently—like so many other things that happened to me in my early years—eventually served as a lesson for me. What we learn is usually a mixed bag of things, good and not so good. We each have our own personal journey. Our roads are unique, with numerous twists and turns.

In hindsight, I realize that I picked up both good and bad habits from my childhood. Without realizing it, I learned how to be resourceful at a young age. But I also adopted counterproductive ways of thinking and doing things that would plague me for a good part of my life.

Scarcity Mindset

> **Matthew 6:25**
>
> *Therefore I say unto you, Take no thought for your life, what ye shall eat, or what ye shall drink; nor yet for your body, what ye shall put on. Is not the life more than meat, and the body than raiment?*

One of the worst traits I adopted from my parents was a mindset of scarcity. Scarcity of the mind is when you are so obsessed with a lack of something—usually time or money—that you can't seem to focus on anything else, no matter how hard you try. I always believed that I didn't have enough and that money and opportunities were limited. This way of thinking cheated me out of achieving bigger and better things. I didn't have the patience to wait. My need for short-term gratification ruled my every move. I jumped from one project to another if I didn't experience results immediately. Making bad and uninformed choices became a trademark of my life.

Instead of making well-thought-out choices, I tended to jump on things that, in the long run, did not serve me well. Many times, I was afraid to make uncomfortable decisions. So, I made many bad choices out of fear. I always felt that my good fortune would run out soon. I was afraid to lose my money, and I never understood what the word abundance meant. I was always in survival mode. I was a firefighter by default. Putting out small fires—often self-imposed emergencies—became a way of life. Treating others with generosity was foreign. I had to hold on to whatever I had, because I was afraid that what I had would run out. Just getting by was enough for me.

Can you relate? Have you battled with this type of thinking and living? I know many people who are afraid to live with reckless abandon, afraid to take risks. They live with the fear of losing what they have, or they believe they won't acquire more than their misconceived fair share.

They hold on to whatever they currently have for dear life. They are good at surviving—but horrible at thriving.

My life story is filled with instances where I fell short of the mark. Don't get me wrong, I did achieve some of my goals. But because of my limiting beliefs, I stopped short before I accomplished significant results. Instead of stretching myself, I settled by playing it safe. I never rocked the boat. I convinced myself to be a good soldier, never upsetting other people with my opinions or challenging them with another point of view. I was more interested in seeking approval and being accepted by others. Unfortunately, holding back my thoughts and opinions negatively affected me by building up anger and resentment. When I was triggered, all hell would break loose. I spent a lifetime reacting. That led me and others into many hardships and unnecessary arguments.

Fueled by Emotions

You and I are fueled by our emotions. We feel every minute of the day. The problem lies in being obsessed with our feelings. When we are ruled by our emotions, we live like slaves. We become self-absorbed. While I was growing up and well into my adult life,

I was a perfectionist. Everything had to be just right—especially my feelings—before I acted. Ironically, this caused me to make more mistakes than if I had just moved forward. I was afraid to fail. Overthinking, which is an acute symptom of being a chronic worrier, kept me stuck. Yet I was also impulsive, doing things without taking the time to objectively think them through. If I was scared and doubtful, I stayed put. Other times, I did things because they made me feel good. This lethal combination was a thorn in my side. I never had balance. I lacked any middle ground. I had core values, but often dismissed them to serve the needs of my feelings. My life was run by a multitude of negative emotions like fear, guilt, anger, sadness, isolation, and loneliness. Fear and guilt ruled over everything I did or didn't do for many years. I was restless, irritable, and discontented. Feeling frustrated was my norm. I acted or didn't act based on how I felt. Feelings ran my life. I was constantly reading my "feelings thermometer."

The following are the negative emotions I suffered from. I believe millions of other are experiencing them as well.

1. **Anger:** Although some anger is warranted—perhaps because of injustices in society or your child misbehaving—most of the anger we experience is really anger toward ourselves. We are angry that we aren't doing things we know we should be doing, or angry that we're doing things we know are wrong—perhaps staying in dysfunctional relationships or bailing out sooner than we should. Or maybe we make hasty decisions based on wrong or not enough information. As we move on in life and become wiser, we can't hide from the truth the way we used to. Our self-awareness moves to the fore, and we can't BS ourselves anymore. If we continue saying or doing the wrong things, our self-directed anger becomes worse.

2. **Anxiety:** A chronic worry habit kills our joy and ruins our lives. Once we develop the habit of compulsive worrying, it's impossible to live a full and happy life. We shortchange ourselves and our loved ones because of our doomsday mindset. We're always ready for the other shoe to drop. For some strange reason, we believe we're thinking and acting more responsibly because we're worrying about what could go wrong. This creates self-inflicted stress.
3. **Guilt:** This feeling plagues our lives dramatically. Of course, if we hurt someone else by what we say or do, we need to be ready to apologize and make amends as soon as possible. However, many people believe they're bad and deserve to endure guilt. We punish ourselves constantly and needlessly. Excessive guilt is rooted in self-loathing, a condition connected to low self-esteem and the twisted belief that we are inferior to others. We beat ourselves up because we aren't perfect.
4. **Sadness:** Unrealistic expectations and life's many disappointments make us sad. Maybe we didn't get the job we wanted or missed out on the new client we chased for months. Maybe a romantic relationship ended or the loss of a loved one or close friend created a deep hole in our soul. All this can be unbearable. In extreme cases, sadness may lead to depression. Unfortunately, way too many people are living their lives in quiet desperation, too proud to seek help.

Isaiah 43:18
Remember ye not the former things, neither consider the things of old.

When we look at our lives, we discover some things about ourselves that we are proud of and some things we are ashamed of. Our tendency is to beat ourselves up because we fell short and weren't perfect. If only we tried harder, things might have turned out better. I have learned that every time I look back at my life, I usually say, "If I would have . . ." or "I could have . . ." or— and this is the worst one—"I should have . . ." All three of these statements are guilt-ridden.

We feel remorse for things we could have said or done differently. When we indulge in regrets over the past, we screw up today and we set ourselves up for a miserable tomorrow. I learned the hard way that when we drive through life constantly looking at the rearview mirror, we'll crash into the future.

Experiencing Growth

Growth can mean different things. We grow emotionally; we grow our minds, our relationships, and our careers. We grow financially, and we grow spiritually. We also grow physically.

I had a significant growth spurt between sixth and seventh grades. By the time I was twelve, I was six feet tall.

I felt very awkward among my friends, who I had surpassed in height. In adolescence, emotional growth usually lags behind physical growth. I felt old beyond my years, so without realizing it, I decided to think and act older than I really was. I cultivated a serious persona, hardly ever smiling. I became reserved and very quiet.

Around this time, I discovered basketball. I was a natural from the beginning, quickly becoming an all-star in middle school. I was immensely popular and was riding on top of the world.

Basketball became my obsession. For the first time in my life, I excelled at something. My talent grew as I entered high school. I was a starter each of my four years in high school. I was good— but I could have been great. I only went as far as I believed I could go.

That was the beginning of a lifetime of only doing so much, never being willing to go the extra step in my development. In retrospect, it was the beginning of a lifelong pattern. I underutilized my talent and potential. I had a mysterious internal obstacle that held me back throughout my life, wasting my God-given gifts. I had all the potential in the world, but I fell short many times over.

Although I underachieved for most of my life, I did achieve some things that I'm very proud of:
- I'm the father of two wonderful kids and three grandsons.
- I was a basketball star in high school.
- I was a pioneer and one of the top sales professionals and trainers in the flower-importing industry in Miami.
- I was a nationally ranked agent and sales manager in the financial services industry.
- I became one of the top economic development leaders in South Florida.
- I'm a pioneer of business talk radio in South Florida.

These accomplishments remind me that although I've fallen short many times, I have been successful in spite of life's challenges. I haven't been a total failure, yet I could have accomplished so much more. My upbringing forced me to retreat into my own fabricated world that protected me from the real world. Remaining in this bubble caused me to remain mediocre, underutilizing my God-given talents and falling short in many aspects of my life—with my family and finances, professionally, and in the community. I wasn't the best version of myself. I continuously sought comfort, unwilling to pay the price. Laziness and lack of discipline and focus drove my processes. I sought the easy road.

The world I created caused me to neglect certain responsibilities, putting off things that needed my attention. Being neglectful caused many unnecessary fires in my life. The responsibilities I postponed eventually caught up with me. Thinking small and settling and an attitude of just getting by built up anger inside me, because I knew deep down that I could do and be better. I lived a life with too many unresolved issues. I was oblivious to the fact that I was keeping myself in a kind of quicksand, stuck and slowly sinking.

Day by Day

Life is a moment by moment experience, progressing one day at a time, one step at a time. I always wanted to get to my destination or achieve my goal *yesterday*, but it never seemed to turn out that way. Everything had to occur according to my timetable.

As far back as I can remember, I have been a very impatient man. In some situations, impatience served me well. Most of the time, however, it harmed me. When I didn't get my way, I became frustrated and angry, absorbed by self-pity. The more I raised my expectations, the more discouraged and disappointed I became. This pattern became more acute as I got older.

In the perfect world I created, a place that was my sanctuary, everything always went my way. I got what I wanted when I wanted it. This world was a mental illusion I fabricated all the way back when I was a young child. Without realizing or understanding what I was doing to myself, I built invisible walls. I deceived myself into believing all was well and would forever remain that way if I was in control. I disconnected from the real world. If my plans didn't work, it was because of outside circumstances beyond my control or it was someone else's fault.

Entitlement ran rampant in my life.

The good news is that, as I progressed in life, I found out I wasn't unique. Millions of people around the world live their lives in a similar way. This kind of disconnection is a symptom of fear and denial.

When I noticed this pattern in my behavior, I became ruthlessly honest with myself and realized I needed to change. I learned that admitting a problem, accepting a disagreeable truth, is only the beginning. To truly shift my attitude, I had to take the next step—take action. My desire to change was positive and honorable, but if I was not willing to do what I needed to do, nothing would be different. I would continue on in the same old way.

I was living an insane life—doing the same thing repeatedly expecting different results. Unfortunately, millions of people throughout the world live their lives exactly like this. But the fact that this is very common is not an excuse for anyone to continue in such madness.

How many of us have prevented ourselves from living a life that fulfills the God-given potential we've had since the moment we were born? Each of us has unique qualities, designed specifically for us. I had enormous God-given gifts: creativity, eloquence, and resourcefulness.

> **Jonah 2:5**
> *The waters compassed me about, even to the soul: the depth closed me round about, the weeds were wrapped about my head.*

I've always had those gifts inside me; unfortunately, I haven't always used them. Why? I'm not totally sure. What I do know is that I had limiting beliefs that held me back. There was no good reason to feel or think the way I did, but it happened. I cheated myself and others by not fulfilling my God-given potential. Have you lived up to your potential or have you fallen short?

Was This As Good as It Gets?

In retrospect, my life was more or less okay. I grew up in a loving family; I wouldn't trade my parents and brothers. My school years were filled with good friends, an excellent education, and athletic success. My professional life had good moments. And most importantly, I helped raise two wonderful kids who make me proud beyond words. I really don't have anything to complain about.

I wasn't famous, but I was well-liked and respected by my friends and professional colleagues. I was a regular guy, though flawed like most people. I had a good life, one that would be envied by many. If anything had happened to me, I would have been remembered as a good guy who made a difference; not perfect, but good enough. My tombstone would read, "A nice, good, and average guy who tried his best."

Fortunately, God had other plans for me. I hadn't fully utilized the multitude of talents gifted to me by God. In the subsequent chapters, I'll explain what his providence and grace did for me. I will share a significant, defining moment, one that started with a profound challenge and eventually led to the greatest victory in my life.

Key Points

- Each of us has a story to tell—how we lived and the challenges and adversity that shaped our lives for better or worse.

- Every one of us has a personal journey. We may relate to others, but our roads are unique, with numerous twists and turns.
- When we indulge in regrets about the past, we screw up today and set up a miserable tomorrow.

Ruthlessly Honest Questions

1. Where is your life right now?

   _____
   _____
   _____
   _____

2. What are you most proud of?

   _____
   _____
   _____
   _____

3. What is the biggest adversity you've experienced, and how did you overcome it?

   _____
   _____
   _____
   _____

4. If you could change one thing about your life, what would it be?

   _____
   _____
   _____
   _____

> *"Change the lenses of your vision to see what you've been missing."*
>
> **—PETE DE LA TORRE**

CHAPTER 2

Wake-Up Call

The beginning of any new year is a celebratory time for all. We are filled with great anticipation and hope, boosted by our annual New Year's resolutions. Our goals are driven by a resolve to enjoy and experience the best year ever. However, as we have come to know, God typically has other plans for us, plans that don't match up with what we desire for ourselves.

As I welcomed in 2021, I had my own set of plans that didn't involve any sort of health challenge. Honestly, I don't think anyone anticipates dealing with medical issues, especially at the start of a new year. Unbeknownst to me, there was something lurking in the dark that was about to shake up my world. I was about to embark on a journey that I didn't plan for and, frankly, never would have made reservations for. Yet God, the great Travel Agent of the universe, had mapped out a new kind of road trip for me.

On January 3, my wife Jacquelyn and I returned home to Miami, Florida from a holiday trip to Nashville, Tennessee.

During the entire two-hour flight in a plane filled to capacity, with people sitting elbow to elbow, I experienced severe pain in my legs—worse pain than I ever remember having. When the plane landed and the passengers began to exit, I struggled to get out of my chair. Once I was able to stand up, I began the long, grueling walk through the airport terminal to baggage claim. After we picked up our luggage, we hailed a taxi to take us to our apartment. Getting into the taxi was a nightmare. I had to grab both my legs to get them into the car. Jacquelyn didn't understand how bad the pain was until she saw what I had to do just to sit down in the taxi. That was a sign of things to come.

During the next couple of weeks, the pain in my legs spread to my shoulders and arms. I didn't get a good night's rest for more than four weeks, barely getting an hour of sleep on any given evening. My energy level and mindset were in the gutter. I completely lost the motivation and anticipation I had on January 1. I began to get very nervous about what was happening to me. The tunnel of uncertainty I experienced was very dark. I finally decided to see a doctor to find out what the hell was going on.

In hindsight, that was one of the most important decisions of my life. Pain can be a strong motivator to get you off your butt and into action. Although I didn't know it at the time, God was working behind the scenes, orchestrating a new path for me that would dramatically transform my life. It was a profound blessing in disguise, beyond my comprehension. I soon found out that God has been, is, and will always be in charge.

After extensive bloodwork, I was diagnosed with polymyalgia rheumatica, an arthritic condition that can affect anyone over fifty years old. The good news was that the ailment wasn't permanent and could disappear in 18–24 months by taking a medication called prednisone, a steroid that alleviates inflammation in the body. Within a few days, I began to feel much better and was able to finally get some much-needed sleep. Although I thought I was out of the woods, God was getting me ready to deal with something much more serious. Within five months, I was under the knife for a life-altering surgery.

When we encounter a serious health challenge or any unwelcome adversity—a moment of utter and paralyzing fear—we can easily freak out. We do our best to muster the courage to face our situation. We ask ourselves, "What does it all mean?" If we are not careful, gloom and doom can reign supreme in mind and spirit. A negative force that I call "the enemy" is ready to attack and pull us into the abyss. It is during these moments that our faith and trust in God is paramount.

With health challenges, we understand that doctors and surgeons with their medical expertise will prescribe medications for our illnesses or perform surgery to heal us. But let's get something straight—God is the ultimate healer.

No human being can heal; that is God's job. His grace and supernatural favor has the power to do things for us that we can never do for ourselves, including ridding our bodies of disease. The good Lord intervened on my behalf, and he can do the same for you if you let him. When you do allow God to be God and don't get in the way, miracles will happen for you beyond your wildest imagination—including, perhaps, the reversal of a disturbing medical report that appears hopeless and terminal.

We sometimes wonder why things happen the way they do and when they do. Many occurrences in our lives are not what we hoped for, expected, or wanted.

For example, we work hard to attain our goals, yet we fall short. We apply for a dream job but don't get it. A romantic relationship doesn't work out, and we're forced to break it off. We pass through an unexpected health crisis. These so-called negative outcomes, as unfavorable and disagreeable as they may be, happen for a reason. They are God's will—he has other plans for us, whether we like it or not.

If you trust God—which can be quite difficult during extreme challenges—keep praying, because eventually, your prayers will be answered.

> **Matthew 7:7**
> *Ask, and it shall be given you; seek, and ye shall find; knock, and it shall be opened unto you.*

Whether you're pleading for healing for your body or for your relationships, finances, or business: Keep praying. God's will is majestic. He is ready to bless you, especially when you are going through a valley of darkness. What happens after the storm has passed may be astonishing. When you look back, you'll be convinced that whatever happened was indeed a blessing in disguise! Only through adversity are some of the deeper lessons of life learned.

Prostate Cancer News

Prostate cancer was not in my plans. The last thing I thought would happen in 2021 was a journey filled with doctor visits, bloodwork, and medical procedures. As I mentioned before, the year started with pain in my legs and shoulders that started out of the blue. These pains caused many sleepless nights, excessive worry, and frustration. The doctor ordered comprehensive bloodwork to include a PSA examination, a laboratory test that measures the amount of prostate-specific antigen (PSA) found in the blood. We discovered two things: I had extremely high levels of inflammation, and I had a very high PSA level of 7.9.

I saw a urologist, Dr. Jason Wolf, one month later. He was concerned about my high PSA level. My PSA score was double what was considered normal for a man my age. After hearing him out, I faced the first what was to be a series of life-changing decisions coming my way in the following two months.

Dr. Wolf explained to me that I had two choices: Get a biopsy or do additional bloodwork to see if my PSA level dropped. I decided to do the bloodwork and check back with the doctor in thirty days to review the results. At my next appointment, I got some bad news—my PSA level had increased to 12.0, three times higher than the normal range. Whatever was going on was happening fast.

At that point, I had no choice but to schedule a biopsy. I had already delayed seeing the urologist for two months, hoping that in some magical way the situation would just disappear. Two weeks after the biopsy, I received the news I was hoping I wouldn't hear—I had prostate cancer! This was my first real encounter with *ruthless honesty*.

When I heard the news, I was frozen with fear. I was stunned in a way I had never experienced before. I know the doctor kept talking, sharing important information with me on how to proceed, but most of it went over my head. I had trouble comprehending anything he said after the moment when I heard the word *cancer*!

Not only did I have cancer, but it was aggressive. I had what the doctor described as a Category 3 malignant tumor. It was a very serious condition, and I didn't have a lot of time to think about my next move. Whatever course of treatment I chose would need to be started within a short time frame.

After regaining my composure, I reviewed my options with the doctor. I had to make what was probably the most important decision of my life to that point—how to treat the cancer. I had two options: Radiation treatment or the removal of my prostate.

After getting a second opinion from another urologist and after having private conversations with friends and family members who had had prostate cancer, I made a monumental decision. I chose to have surgery to remove my prostate. Both options had similar success rates. However, the aggressiveness of the cancer was evident. I felt that it was wiser to have the surgery in the hope that the cancer was contained in the prostate and had not spread.

Finding out the truth is imperative. Far too often, we're in such a rush to get an answer now that we act on misinformation. This can lead to wrong decisions, decisions that we eventually pay a steep price for.

When I heard my cancer diagnosis, I needed facts about my condition and how to treat it effectively. I couldn't afford to jump the gun. My mission was to reach out to the right sources— in this case, other cancer specialists—to consider all my options. I wanted the raw truth regarding my condition, without any beating around the bush. I was not looking for answers that would make me feel good. I wanted the truth! When cancer is staring you down, you need to stare back at it with a vengeance. You cannot accept defeat.

An important step in resolving a problem is to get the facts and at all costs avoid opinions that aren't grounded in the truth. Fortunately, I had two proven treatment options at my disposal: Radiation or surgical removal of my prostate. Both had similar success rates of approximately 85%–90%. However, as I mentioned previously, my cancer was growing fast and was on the brink of breaking through the walls of the prostate and spreading to other parts of my body. That would have been a "Category 5" situation, with a possibility of catastrophic damage. I needed to eradicate the cancer while it was isolated in my prostate.

We encounter many problems that start small, like a tropical storm. If we don't take care of the problem in its early stages, it may spread and become a much larger problem. A once-isolated issue can grow into a monster that can ruin relationships, businesses, and health.

Surgery to remove my prostate would result in a necessary organ being removed from my body. I knew that the aftermath of the surgery could be traumatic and life-changing—but so could the possibility of death. Putting a Band-Aid on anything involving our health is typically a short-term solution that's doomed to fail. I did not want to deal with this cancer down the road; the time to get rid of it was *now*. I had to put on my big-boy pants and face the wrath or suffer the consequences later.

After a short period of reflection and prayer, it was time to put on my seat belt and get ready for the ride of my life. I knew that the course of action I was about to embark on would affect me for the rest of my life. In my research, which included speaking to close friends and my older brother—people who had also experienced prostate cancer—provided me with direction and allowed to me to make an informed decision. One thing was for sure: I was not going to do it my way. This situation was way over my head, and the last time I looked, I wasn't a medical doctor. God knows I had made decisions that weren't based on valid information. There were many times when I had jumped the gun in my haste to get things over with. I had been a tad impatient, if you know what I mean!

I needed to decide on whatever proven treatment was necessary to take care of this health crisis. There wouldn't be any shortcuts or new, exotic, or enlightening healing plans for me. I wasn't going to play with fire, because I wasn't in the mood to get burned. After gathering the facts and spending time in deep prayer, I decided to take aggressive action to fight an aggressive cancer. I scheduled my surgery for five weeks later. What followed was a roller coaster of emotions leading up to the big day!

Life often serves us unexpected curve balls. They seem to come out of nowhere, without any notification. What happens when we find ourselves on a detour? How long do we stay off course? How do we gather ourselves and get back on the right track?

I am eternally grateful that I ended up with polymyalgia. This illness prompted me to visit the doctor. Without the polymyalgia, I would have avoided seeing the doctor, just as I had typically done through the years. I've always had the fear that the doctor would find something wrong with me. In this case, I did have something wrong, and, boy, was I lucky. God's alarm clock was a deafening one that I couldn't ignore, because if I had, I would have needed a tombstone.

When we look back on our lives, we find that God sends us messages and insights about things we need to change or do differently, issues or opportunities we can't dismiss. Yet so many of us either miss the messages or don't acknowledge them.

Neglect—a bad habit of mine—eventually caught up with me. As much as we try to evade responsibilities, they eventually catch up with us. When they do, it may be too late. A perfect example of being neglectful is not dealing with or taking our health seriously. So many people have convinced themselves that all is and will remain good. Millions of people eat the wrong food and hardly ever exercise. Obesity plagues the US at alarming rates.

Experiencing polymyalgia rheumatica was a clear-cut blessing in disguise. It probably saved my life. When we encounter a new problem, we need to accept the reality of the problem before anything can change. We need time to allow the new reality to settle in. Only then can we consider what the next steps may be. We fully understand that waiting for the right solution will not work. Once we decide on what to do next, we must take action—the right action! It doesn't matter what the issue is—with health, finances, business, or family—we need to take action. No one is immune to suffering and adversity.

> **Job 5:7**
> *Yet man is born unto trouble, as the sparks fly upward.*

We feel pressure from wants, needs, sorrows, persecution, unpopularity, and loneliness. Some people suffer for things they've done; others suffer because of what people do to them. Many suffer because they are victims of circumstances beyond their control.

I believe the cancer experience mimics life. When you have cancer, you're faced with a terrible and frightening reality, one that hits you at your core. Words cannot describe the chaos of emotions you feel when confronted with this life-shattering diagnosis. You feel powerless and vulnerable. You can react with the proverbial "Why me?" and sulk in self-pity, or you can respond with a why-not-me? attitude.

No one is immune from health challenges; they'll happen, sooner or later. Life is full of adversity, and that adversity sometimes includes bad medical news. A realistic, positive attitude—"I will face this and do whatever is necessary"—is the first and most important step in overcoming any dilemma, whether it's a health crisis or some other kind. When you decide that failure is not an option, your determination and resolve become the catalyst for a favorable outcome.

We all come to crossroads in our lives, moments of uncertainty about what to do next. We understand that a change is needed; we know that things won't and can't remain the same. These important decisions test our courage. We can go right, left, or stay put. Not doing anything may prevent us from going to the next level in our personal growth, career, or relationships—or, more importantly, with our health. For me, the uncertainty of being diagnosed with cancer was beyond sobering. I had a Category 3 tumor. When a Category 3 hurricane hits, there's usually major damage and a potential for loss of life. When you have a malignant tumor in the prostate, you need to "board up" the rest of your body to prevent the cancer from spreading and creating a Category 5 scenario, one that could be the kiss of death. I was swimming in deep, uncharted waters, having never experienced any sort of health issue like this.

The word *cancer* is, without a doubt, the scariest word in the English language. Or in any language, period. The reality of it hit me square between the eyes. As soon as the news settled in, it was time to do something about it—quickly. The cancer required my undivided attention. A nondecision, maintaining the status quo, would have been deadly. I was forced to make a choice regarding how to proceed. The cancer motivated me to act. The question was, what should I do? Taking care of my health instantly became my top priority. For the time being, everything else in my life was a distant second.

> **Jeremiah 6:16**
> *Thus saith the Lord, Stand ye in the ways, and see, and ask for the old paths, where is the good way, and walk therein, and ye shall find rest for your souls. But they said, We will not walk therein.*

Some of the choices we face in life are scary and uncomfortable to consider. One wrong decision can be life-altering. Understanding our priorities—what's really important to us and our loved ones—is nonnegotiable. Undoubtedly, the number-one priority in our lives is our health, because without our health, nothing else matters. Sooner or later, we all face momentous decisions regarding our health, whether we like it or not. When that time comes, do your research, talk with the right people, and take time to pray. I assure you that you will make the right choice, one that will benefit you in ways you cannot imagine.

Key Points
- God typically has plans for us that don't match up with what we desire for ourselves.
- Some of the deeper lessons of life are learned only through adversity.
- Putting a Band-Aid on something in our lives—especially when it involves our health— typically is a short-term solutions that's doomed to fail.

Ruthlessly Honest Questions
1. How do you deal with adversity?
   _____
   _____
   _____

2. How have you handled previous challenges in your life?
   _____
   _____
   _____

3. How do you respond when things don't go as planned?
   _____
   _____
   _____
   _____

4. Do you get angry with God when he doesn't answer your prayers in the way or at the time you want?
   _____
   _____
   _____
   _____

―――――――――――――――――――⚫―――――――――――――――――――

*"During moments of enormous doubt
and confusion, you are waking up.
Don't go back to sleep."*

―PETE DE LA TORRE

―――――――――――――――――――⚫―――――――――――――――――――

PART II

Marching Orders from God

CHAPTER 3
My Self-Discovery

God Is Great and All-Powerful

On July 7, 2021, D-Day had arrived: The day of my surgery. I woke up early that morning, while it was still dark. I took some time to pray and meditate on what I was about to walk into. I knew that God was guiding and protecting me each step of the way.

After arriving at the hospital and going through the preoperative procedures, I was wheeled into the operating room. The anesthesia put me in a state of euphoria. I felt an amazing sense of peace, and deep down inside, I believed all would be well.

The next thing I knew, I was in the recovery room after a two-hour operation. Next, I was taken to my room to begin recovering from the surgery. After getting settled in, I found out that my operation had been a success. The surgeon and his team had removed the prostate in time, and the cancer had not metastasized. However, I was told that, as a precaution, I might need radiation treatment.

A week later, I reviewed the post-surgery pathology report with Dr. Wolf and learned that I was 100% cancer-free and didn't need any further treatment. I was on top of the world. The gratitude and relief I felt was indescribable. After six weeks of uncertainty and anxiety, the ordeal was over.

Now that I had overcome cancer, the coast was clear; perhaps I could go on with my life, thanking God for his help and carrying on as the same guy I had been for 63 years. I could think and do things as I always had, with the same mindset that had filled my life with mediocrity.

But no, I couldn't.

When I acknowledged all the facts about my ailment and remembered the whirlwind of emotions I felt, there was no way I could stay the same. The cancer wake-up call impacted me beyond what I could have ever imagined. The fear and uncertainty I experienced pierced through me.

The lightning strike of cancer jolted me to my very core. It was God's way of saying, "Welcome to the real world." It was a sudden dose of ruthless honesty thrust upon me. God lost his patience and decided it was time for me to break out of my comfort zone.

Recapturing the past would have been a total waste of time. I started asking myself questions I had never considered but needed to address.

What was the first step I needed to take to move forward? Where would that step take me? I knew that God had given me a second chance, so I needed to do something different in my life. But what? If God had pulled me through my illness, what was the plan? What did it all mean? He had protected and guided me throughout life's journey, so why would I question his plans now?

Actually, God saved me twice within four months. Early in November 2021, Jacquelyn and I visited Charlotte, North Carolina, for a short vacation. On our last day, we decided to have breakfast in the downtown area. We walked through the streets, enjoying the brisk weather and friendly smiles. After breakfast, we started walking back to our rental car. On the way, we stopped at a traffic light, waiting for a green light to cross the intersection. As we were about to step off the sidewalk, a speeding black pickup truck came out of nowhere and passed within inches of running us over. If not for the hand of God, both of us might have been killed or seriously injured. It was another near-death experience, though this one would have been instant. The profound scare we experienced can hardly be expressed in words. To say that the incident affected us profoundly is a gross understatement. We were numb for the rest of the day and during our flight back home.

When we are in harm's way—whether it's due to bad choices or simply being in the wrong place at the wrong time—God's majestic arms embrace and protect us. When we are confronted with death, our lives flash before us. It's amazing how many scenes cross our mind in a split second.

I can give many examples of times when God has pulled me through one challenge after another. When bad things happen, many people believe that God is punishing them. Nothing could be farther from the truth. If you truly believe in him, you will understand that whatever adversity we encounter happens for a reason. Sometimes we understand what's going on, but many times we don't see why *this* challenge and why *now*. Sometimes events are so troubling that we can't see how they might be a part of God's plan for our lives.

> "God will not permit any troubles to come upon us unless he has a specific plan by which great blessings can come out of the difficultly."
> —Peter Marshall

> **Ephesians 2:8-9:**
> *For by grace are ye saved through faith; and that not of yourselves: it is the gift of God: not of works, lest any man should boast.*

When we take time to look back at our lives, we recognize that in every event, it was God's hands and power that pulled us through. We can clearly see that it was his presence that guided us through turbulent times. It's ironic to think that, when the next challenge arrives, we may somehow believe we're doomed and that, this time around, God will abandon us. So many people have a short-term memory and forget that, no matter what, we will be saved—especially when we still have work to do, as per God's plans for us. If God allowed cancer to afflict me at that particular time and place in my life, then I have to believe there was a reason, *his* reason.

During such times, we may find it difficult to trust God completely—yet trust him we must.

The best way for any of us to try to understand life as it unfolds is to realize and accept that there is a time for everything. It is guaranteed that we will experience different seasons, ups and downs, twists and turns.

> **Ecclesiastes 3:1-8**
>
> *To every thing there is a season, and a time to every purpose under the heaven: A time to be born, and a time to die;*
>
> *A time to plant, and a time to pluck up that which is planted; A time to kill, and a time to heal;*
>
> *A time to break down, and a time to build up; A time to weep, and a time to laugh;*
>
> *A time to mourn, and a time to dance;*
>
> *A time to cast away stones, and a time to gather stones together; A time to embrace, and a time to refrain from embracing;*
>
> *A time to get, and a time to lose;*
>
> *A time to keep, and a time to cast away; A time to rend, and a time to sew;*
>
> *A time to keep silence, and a time to speak; A time to love, and a time to hate;*
>
> *A time of war, and a time of peace.*

A surefire way to build our trust in God is to seek an ongoing connection with him. Whether we realize it or not, he is constantly connecting with us. He is always reminding us that he loves us and truly wants the very best for us and our families. The problem is that we're often tuned out and don't listen. We block out his insight and wisdom. As a result, we miss out on living a life of abundance and purpose.

God's communication with us is the truth. He lets us know with ruthless honesty the life he expects us to live. The problem is that when we depend on our own thinking and interpretation, we do things that are harmful to us. We associate with people and put ourselves in situations that do not serve us. We fail to understand that we must disconnect from what does not serve us. When it doesn't feel right, that is God telling us to go in another direction.

We all ask the same question: Why did God put me here? It's a simple question to ask and, at times, a very complicated question to answer. As you seek to discover (or, perhaps, rediscover) God's plan for your life, start by remembering this: You are here because God put you here, and he did so for a very good reason. When you discover God's plan for your life, you will experience abundance, peace, joy, and power—God's power.

Self-Reflection

I believe without a shadow of a doubt that I have marching orders from God, especially because he saved me from cancer. He has clearly stated that I should work in his name for the benefit of my family, friends, the business world, and the community. He gave me gifts, and it is time for me to finally use them.

However, before I began this work, God wanted me to pause and reflect on what the cancer was really about. To make my reflections a positive and productive experience, I had to have an open mind and let go of any preconceived ideas.

I took a hard look at the big picture. I couldn't afford to discard or dismiss anything. I discovered many things about myself, some good, and some not so good. The following are some key revelations:

- I had more faith in God than I had previously thought.
- I had the potential to do much more in my life by utilizing my God-given abilities and talents.
- My family and friends loved me deeply.
- I had the power to grow as a person.
- I needed to change some things so that I could be the best version of myself.
- I could not continue neglecting the important things in life. Taking shortcuts was no longer an option.
- I had to connect with my core values and live by them.
- I was not taking care of my health as I should.
- I needed to have an open mind. I was cheating myself and others of what life had to offer.

A time of self-reflection allows us to take a step back and gain perspective on what matters most and what must be ignored. Through self-reflection, we understand what we need to disconnect from. In addition, we can process events and see them clearly. As we think back on and learn from our experiences, we construct new knowledge and apply it to new experiences.

God had given me certain gifts that I had underutilized. It was time to step up to the plate and begin swinging away. Although I've long known that God created each of us unique, with special talents, I underplayed my gifts because of my limiting beliefs.

Most of the time, I've been a person who had things figured out. What I didn't realize is that God has always been working behind the scenes, pulling strings, guiding and inspiring me. It was time to pay attention.

The Ruthlessly Honest Truth of Ruthless Honesty

The nuggets we discover during an exercise in self-reflection are priceless. If you proceed with a fully open mind, you will discover things that were hidden. You'll face the absolute truth about yourself, and it may be hard to accept.

Digging deep inside ourselves can be a sobering experience. It takes courage and determination to face what is revealed. The good news is that we also uncover great qualities and talents we've always had but have been suppressed due to limiting beliefs. This can be a game changer, but there's one caveat: You must be ruthlessly honest with yourself each step of the way. Let's take a closer look at the idea of ruthless honesty.

Living a lie is bad. Big lies bring about bad things, but white lies do, too. The problem with white lies is that they look harmless. We convince ourselves that it's no big deal to tell white lies.

The longer you evade the truth, the more your life will be run by negative emotions like fear, anger, frustration, and anxiety. These emotions create inner conflict that eventually catches up with you. Being in this state causes you to be distracted. It may hold you back from being the best version of yourself or create unnecessary stress that results in a disease or other hardships.

In work and life, it's advantageous to be clear and honest about what we're doing or saying at any given moment—in our interactions with others, with ourselves, and our environment. To be honest with others, we first need to be honest with ourselves; otherwise, we're cheating ourselves.

Millions of people are living what I call a fake life. Social media provides perfect examples of this. Countless people are constantly uploading photos portraying a so-called perfect life in which all is wonderful, all the time! I think we all know that it's BS.

Due to the growing global political virus, millions of people are chastised for speaking their minds. If you express your honest opinions, you are blocked off from society. As a result, many keep their mouths shut for fear of being ridiculed and reprimanded.

Ruthless self-honesty is not easy. It takes a lot of practice to be appropriately ruthless. I examine myself every day. I've noticed that some of my activities are still smoke and mirrors— I'm doing things just for the sake of doing them, so I can cross them off my list.

Toward the end of the movie *A Few Good Men*, there's a classic scene where Lieutenant Daniel Kaffee (Tom Cruise) is deposing Colonel Nathan R. Jessup (Jack Nicholson). He makes a bold request: "I want the truth." The colonel answers bluntly with, "You can't handle the truth!"

Being ruthlessly honest is sometimes hard to handle. At times, the truth hurts—yet it must be revealed. Therefore, many people—including me—would rather not face the reality of some situations. But it can be disastrous to continue hiding from what we know to be true.

It is incumbent upon us to understand that truth is fact, not opinion. Truth isn't what we *wish* things could be; truth is what things *are*. The more we face the reality of a situation, the more free we become and the more joy and success we'll experience in every area of our lives.

Freedom

Everyone longs to be free, living peacefully and abundantly—this is a universal desire. Many people enjoy the freedom to live their lives as they wish. But sadly, many others live in societies that prevent them from enjoying these freedoms.

Yet there's a freedom that anyone, anywhere, can have at any time, a freedom with a value that can't be quantified. It's the freedom to be your true self. This can only be attained when you live a life of ruthless honesty.

In many cases, the freedom to be your true self is ignited by adversity, when you face a harsh reality you cannot avoid or ignore, when you have no choice but to act or perish. When you confront and resolve the problem, you can move forward with a new sense of confidence, knowing that you can face future challenges that come your way—and knowing that you have the freedom to live an authentic life and do amazing things in the future. You're brutally honest with yourself and others. You have no fear of judgment or vulnerability. Your aura of freedom and authenticity is hard to match. You're living to your full potential, without wasting time.

When you are ruthlessly honest, you free yourself from a self-imposed prison and unlock the handcuffs that hold you back. Your connect effectively and authentically with others, with a clear purpose.

Connecting with ruthless honesty is the key to life and business. It provide us with the freedom we have long sought.

People Need People, the Right Ones

I mentioned in Chapter 1 that I lived most of my life isolated from other people. I was a loner. That's a ruthlessly honest truth.

When unexpected adversity or a sudden crisis is thrown upon us, we realize that we desperately need support and assurance from key people. We need family and friends who are there for us, no matter what, people that always have our back.

In the summer of 2021, I was overwhelmed by unimaginable love and support. I wasn't surprised to hear from my kids, my brothers, my cousins, and longtime close friends, but I was taken aback by the outreach of other friends, acquaintances, colleagues, and community leaders. I hadn't heard from some of them in a long time, but they sent their prayers and support before and after my surgery.

I couldn't have gone into the scary and uncertain battle with cancer on my own. The beautiful song "People," by Barbara Streisand, resonates with me: "People who need people are the luckiest people in the world." We all need people who genuinely care for us and will stop at nothing to be with us in a crisis. My cup runs over with inexpressible gratitude I cannot repay. How fortunate I was to have so many people care for me and my well-being! I received a priceless outpouring of love.

I was in the hospital for a day and a half. It was an experience I'll never forget—not because of the surgery and recovery, but because of the small group of people who visited me. I know it sounds cheesy, but it was a genuine love fest. I'm profoundly grateful that my son Michael, my surviving brothers Richie and Phil, my sister-in-law Mirta, and my cousin Frank made the time to be with me. Part of the magic of that time was my brother Richie's unexpected visit. It caught me off guard, because he rarely travels, especially since the outbreak of Covid-19. But he made an overnight trip from Las Vegas and surprised me.

Shining in the middle of all of this was a special someone who took me by the hand and showered me with unconditional love and care that blew me away: My wife, my sweetheart, my love, Jacquelyn.

She has been and is the most important person to me on this journey. Not only is she the love of my life, but she's also my personal nurse. Her tender loving care for me is something I treasure beyond words. I am in awe of her hunger for research, especially on medical topics. Because I'm a bit of a hypochondriac, the last thing I need is to read about serious medical conditions. If I do, it's a safe bet that I'll convince myself that I have whatever I just read about. Jacquelyn's urge to learn has been a huge reason for my rapid recovery.

I also need to take a moment and give kudos to my surgeon, Dr. Wolf. His guidance and matter-of-fact approach was essential and timely. I heard what I needed to hear, even though I didn't necessarily want to hear it. Learning that you have an aggressive cancer is never welcome news. My doctor supported me with the facts, and for that I am eternally and humbly grateful.

My fondest desire for you is that you clearly understand and appreciate that you are a person who needs people. No matter what your circumstances and challenges are, it's ridiculous to go it solo. Believing you can handle tough times by yourself is a surefire way to die a slow death, especially when you're in an emotional pressure cooker. If you have family and close friends in your life, embrace them, love them, appreciate them, and never hold back from reaching out to them in your time of need. Everyone needs people. We can't enjoy or even make it through life alone. I promise you that if you reach out, your loved ones will be by your side every step of the way!

> **Proverbs 17:17**
> *A friend loveth at all times, and a brother is born for adversity.*

We are not meant to live in isolation, to be on an island. Each one of us should have friends who can help us make the right decisions and restore us when we've made wrong ones. We all have blind spots, areas where we need others to help us see. Pride and temptation can keep us from seeing the truth. When we rely on others for guidance and wisdom, we find the strength to be holy.

A word of caution: Make sure the people in your lives are authentic and honest and possess values similar to yours. The last thing we need is to be surrounded by people who suck the life out of us, that don't have our best interests at heart. I call people like that "takers." When you call on them at a time of need, they are nowhere to be found. When things are going well, they flock to you like birds. Keep them away at all costs. Make it a priority to guard your circle of friends.

If you are authentic, living a life of ruthless honesty, and honoring your core values, you will attract like-minded and like-hearted people to your side. God will bring the right people into your life and keep them close to you, especially when you need them most.

Key Points

- When we are in harm's way—either because of our bad choices or because we were at the wrong place at the wrong time—God's majestic arms embrace and protect us.
- It is guaranteed that we will experience different seasons, ups and downs, twists and turns.
- When you are ruthlessly honest, you free yourself from your self-imposed prison and unlock the handcuffs holding you back.

Ruthlessly Honest Questions

1. How well do you know yourself?
   _____
   _____
   _____
   _____

2. Can you handle the truth?
   _____
   _____

3. How often do you connect with family and friends?

4. Do you understand what real freedom means?

"Of all the gifts you've received from God, how many have you unwrapped?"

—PETE DE LA TORRE

CHAPTER 4
New Philosophy

Newfound Treasure

> **Ezekiel 36:26**
> *A new heart also will I give you, and a new spirit will I put within you: and I will take away the stony heart out of your flesh, and I will give you an heart of flesh.*

I got a wake-up call from cancer, and my subsequent intense self-discovery has brought me into a new reality. I was given a newfound treasure—a clean bill of health and a powerful opportunity to restart my life.

I've been enlightened by critical insights, and I've had important questions answered.

As I mentioned in Chapter 2, the entire cancer ordeal, although very frightening, was a massive blessing in disguise. God gave me a second chance at life. I now have a completely different outlook on life and what it really means. The freshness and excitement I feel is exhilarating.

Everything that once seemed impossible is now possible. Being free to be who I've always wanted to be (and should have been) is no longer a pipe dream. God gave me the green light to step on the accelerator and drive forward with confidence and purpose. I've been empowered to make a positive and meaningful impact on my family, friends, business, and community.

This new outlook is great, but as I emerged from my cancer ordeal, I was compelled to ask myself the most critical question of all: "Now what?" What was I supposed to do with my new revelations? How should I to use them? What should my next steps be?

In a short period of time, I had made a bold and life-changing decision. I had acted on the news of my cancer diagnosis—I moved forward with my surgery and recovery and was ready to deal with the long-term consequences of the operation. But afterward, I realized that this was only the beginning, the start of the rest of my life. I was inspired to adopt a new personal philosophy driven by ruthless honesty, one that would my personal foundation as I moved forward.

Embracing a new philosophy is not easy, but it can be done. It requires going back to basics and learning what is real, right, and productive. I had to take charge of my mindset. I had to be someone who follows the teachings of Jesus Christ. His grace provided me with elevated wisdom, perspective, and discernment that I hadn't possessed at any other time in my life.

Without the cancer, I may never have reached this new level of enlightenment.

The adversity I encountered changed everything. It was a special delivery from God, and I couldn't allow this "package" to sit unopened. I had to take out the contents and use them. I now owned an amazing toolbox filled with everything I needed to build a new life.

The spiritual tablet I received was very explicit and ruthlessly honest. It clearly spelled out the steps I needed to take and the exact order I needed to take them in. It was time to discard once and for all the distractions and resistance I had succumbed to for so long. The cost of neglecting my responsibility would be more painful than ever. Once you know the ruthlessly honest truth, you cannot even consider repeating past behavior.

It was game time, and I was inspired to win. I could not afford to lose this one. I was determined to have winning seasons for the remainder of my life. I knew I would have setbacks, that my life's game plan would need retooling along the way. But I would address that when necessary. The point was to score and win!

Reconnecting with Ourselves

When a sports team begins a new season, they have an opportunity for a fresh start. Prior to the start of the season, before any of the games are played, there is an annual ritual that's repeated every year—training camp. The objective is to revisit and retrain on the fundamentals of the sport, to reconnect with the team's goals and objectives for the coming year. Training camp also includes an assessment to find out if the players are in shape, both mentally and physically. This is needed to ensure that the team is ready for the battles ahead.

The game of life runs the same way. Every time we get up in the morning, we are starting a new day. We have a fresh start, a time to reconnect with God and ourselves, reflecting on the day ahead. We can prepare ourselves by reviewing our intentions and strategies. With a well- thought-out plan, we begin each new day with the opportunity to make things happen. We ask ourselves: What kind of day am I going to have today? Am I ready for what's in store for me?

We don't have the answers to these questions, so we humbly ask God to inspire us, guide us, and correct us as we go about our day.

What I'm about to share with you are the elements of the special package God delivered to me, a manual tool set containing direct orders from God. It's a divinely written set of instructions that can provide you with the freedom to succeed in life and in business, a winning formula powered by ruthless honesty and hope:

- YOUR big vision.
- Think BIGGER.
- CLAIM ownership.
- MAKE decisions.
- TAKE action

YOUR Vision

Close your eyes for a few moments and picture this: It's exactly one year from this date. What do you see? What do you want to see? What do you want to have? What do want to be doing? Where do you want to be? How does it feel?

This vision sets the tone for everything that happens next. When you look at the future while connecting with your inner self, tapping into your fondest desires, you ignite a spark that will inspire you. Your desires are placed there by God himself. This awesome realization can revolutionize the rest of your life. Whatever you desire most will have the fuel to manifest in ways that you have only dreamed about.

The key element is emotional connection. Your vision and goals will only become real when you have a personal emotional stake in them. The future you desire must be bigger than whatever you are experiencing at present. Whatever you think about today sets up your tomorrow. In other words, your tomorrow is created today. When you get off track, revert back to your vision and what you desire.

You may have multiple visions and goals—perhaps one for your family and one for your company. These are important, but the vision that matters most is the one you have for yourself. That's the one that provides the most motivation. It will become the number-one reason you get up in the morning.

The vision is yours, not anyone else's. I heard many years ago that if I'm not right with myself, I won't be any good for anyone else. Remember to begin with yourself. If we're ruthlessly honest with ourselves, then we must follow our unique paths.

I cannot live a life that is subservient to the dreams and goals of others, including my family. Appeasing others creates unnecessary frustration and resentment for many people; I know it has for me. Remember, as Shakespeare wrote, "To thine own self be true."

Congruent to creating your personal vision and goals is recognizing and having clarity regarding the mission you're on and why you're on it. What do you hope to accomplish in the pursuit of your goals? What are the objectives and action steps required for success? What impact do you want to have on your family, your business, and your community?

Your mission is an ongoing process, not a one-hit wonder; it never stops. God is constantly on a mission to shower us with his blessings and do his wonderful work for us. Since he never stops, why should we? Our quest should progress, one step at a time, one day at a time. Purpose is pursued, not programmed. It is a manual process, not an automatic process. We must qualify each day.

> **Proverbs 3:5-6**
> Trust in the Lord with all thine heart; and lean not unto thine own understanding. In all thy ways acknowledge him, and he shall direct thy paths.

When someone asks what's important to you, how do you respond? Do you really know what drives you each day? What do you value most? Reach down deep inside and seek to understand the reason for your existence; pray for wisdom and understanding.

Our minds do not determine our core values; that's the function of our hearts. Truth is in our hearts; that's where the Spirit of God resides. Connecting with him as many times as necessary each day will confirm what is really important to us and keep our core values continuously in sight. These nonnegotiable values keep us on the right path. When we hit a detour, they show us how to get back on track. Our core values build our character as we live a life dominated by respect, humility, and love for others, a life that's influenced by the presence of God in all that we think, say, and do. What is most important is how we think—that's where it all starts and ends.

Think BIGGER

Whether we realize it or not, we are all visionaries. At some point each day, our minds drift into the future, thinking about what might happen. We have goals or New Year's resolutions each January 1. Most of us work in order to pay our bills and hopefully take a vacation now and then. A big motivation (and source of anxiety) is our love for our families. We want to make sure we are protecting and providing for them. As a result, millions of people live lives of quiet desperation ruled by mediocrity. They don't know any better; or, if they do, they don't do anything about it.

Thinking bigger sounds great to us. We fantasize about living a wonderful life, being financially independent, traveling to exotic destinations, and owning a beautiful home. It *sounds* wonderful, but when we look around, few (or none) of these things are a reality. Every time we come down from the cloud, reality strikes us a cruel blow. The disappointment we feel is hard to bear, so we retreat into believing these things will never happen for us.

The world is filled with people who are shortchanging themselves by adhering to limiting beliefs—ideas typically adopted in childhood. In some cases, they live with these limiting beliefs for their entire lives, refusing to understand that their way of being can indeed be shifted. Here are some of the most common limiting beliefs:

- I'm not good enough.
- I'm too old or too young.
- I don't have enough time.
- I'm not smart enough.
- I don't have enough experience.
- I'll never be successful.
- I don't have enough money.
- I'll never be one of the best.
- I'm not talented enough.

Do any of these sound familiar?

When people fall into these traps, they imprison themselves in a life of mediocrity. They see others succeed but have no clue how to achieve success. For some strange reason, they think they have bad luck and that it will always be that way. Their reality is an overwhelming feeling of being stuck, entrapped. They need the keys to unlock the door to freedom. The good news is that we already have the keys in our possession.

The keys are with yourself and your mindset. Your beliefs determine your thinking, and based on your thinking, you take action; then, your actions determine your results. Whatever your reality is today is based on the actions you've taken (or not taken). The results you've experienced are the byproduct of this process.

Limiting beliefs > Thinking > Actions > Results

At this point, you may be saying, "Great, thank you for the information. But what I need is to understand why these beliefs exist. How do I get rid of them?"

Why the beliefs are there is not important. They're formed in our minds and have no substance; they are groundless. What you need to do is review your life and uncover the role your limiting beliefs have played in determining the quality of your life. Reverse engineer the process to identify limiting beliefs:

Results > Actions > Thinking > Limiting beliefs

Look at your results and identify the actions that led you there. What kind of thinking led to those actions? Now that you're aware of your thinking, you can identify your limiting beliefs.

> **Job 36:11**
> If they obey and serve him, they shall spend their days in prosperity, and their years in pleasures.

Once you are clear that God did not create you to settle for less, you'll recognize that you must do whatever it takes to achieve your full potential.

Doing whatever it takes means elevating your mindset. The "Altitude of your Attitude" is your first priority. You should aspire to become a "World Class Thinker, a person who focuses on solving problems and finding opportunities. Some of this mindset include:

- Separating truth from facts, operating from objective reaity, and embracing ruthless honesty
- Knowing that adversity is an opportunity to grow and become better
- Choosing discipline over pleasure
- Being decisive
- Taking responsibility
- Taking risks and not being afraid to make mistakes

At all costs, avoid being either a mediocre thinker (desiring security and making survival a priority) or, worse yet, being a person who has a victim mentality. It's your call!

Once you have arrived at this juncture, it's your birthright to take charge, knowing you have a green light and blessing from God—marching orders to move forward and lay claim to the life you're deserving of—with one caveat: You must earn it.

CLAIM Ownership

Taking charge of your life is the biggest responsibility you have. Once you understand that "If it's to be, it's up to me," you're on the pathway to real freedom and the life you desire. No one has the power to change or fix you, and you can't do this for others, either.

The state of your life today is the result of all the patterns of thinking and behaviors you've developed up to this point in your life. If you want a better tomorrow, it is your responsibility to think the right thoughts and do the right things. If you leave it to others, you will succumb to their way of thinking and beliefs, but worst of all, you will give away your God-given power. You'll end up blaming others for the shortcomings in your life—that's exactly what is happening in the world today.

Millions of people live their lives pointing fingers at everyone but themselves for the difficulties they endure. It's all over the news and social media. Many have allowed economic, social, and political pressures to affect their lives negatively. We recently experienced the Covid-19 virus; now we have a more dangerous disease infecting our lives: The blaming virus. When you are overcome by limiting beliefs, low self-esteem, and self-pity, the obvious and easiest thing to do is pass on the blame. Why is this happening at such an alarming rate? In my opinion, the main reason is because of a gross lack of leadership.

Have you heard the phrase, "Too many chiefs and not enough Indians"? Presently, we have the opposite going on: Too many Indians and not enough chiefs. Take a hard look at the world—the business world, society, government, or the family. More people are followers than ever before. Many people accept life as it is, without questioning anything, doing what others are telling them to do or doing what others are doing—even if it isn't the right thing to do. We have a major leadership void today, a lack of those special individuals who live by nonnegotiable core values—leaders who are courageous, willing to think for themselves, and boldly take charge in doing the right things for themselves, their families, and society. What kind of person are you?

Never relinquish your leadership to another person. Never leave the fulfillment of your vision in the hands of others. Make it a priority to master and lead yourself. Consistently humble yourself; strive to grow as a person, and be willing to be a beginner each day. Remind yourself that the buck stops with you and no one else. Man or woman up; put on your big-boy or big-girl pants.

Accountability is not consequences, but ownership. By being accountable and taking ownership, you move from resistance to empowerment, from limits to possibilities, and from mediocrity to greatness.

MAKE Decisions

> *"You cannot make progress without making decisions."*
> **—Jim Rohn**

The core message is this chapter is about making decisions. Once you have been exposed to new ideas, revelations, or knowledge, you must decide what to do with what you've learned.

In my case, I discovered many important things through my cancer ordeal and subsequent healing. My body was healed by God, but so were my soul and spirit. A tidal wave of new possibilities were presented to me. I found new power to make decisions, to make changes in my life. I started by adopting a new philosophy that I knew *could be* the ticket to achieving everything I ever wanted in my life. But if I was to bring these divine insights into reality, I had to make decisions and take action. Sitting back and doing nothing wouldn't change anything. To make progress, I had to *decide* to do it.

You'll move forward and make decisions based on what you believe is important. Regardless of what happens next and whether you realize it or not, you have made a decision. This leads me to believe that we are making decisions all the time. We need to become vigilant about our choices; they are not to be taken lightly.

The quality of our lives is contingent on how we think and the decisions we make. We cannot fool ourselves into thinking that small, insignificant decisions we make are no big deal. *All* decisions matter, especially the small ones we make throughout each day. The accumulation of hundreds of small decisions creates long-lasting effects on our lives. I constantly asked myself, "What is the next right thing to do?" I need this ongoing reminder to ensure that I'm making the best possible decisions on any given day.

At this point, I'd like to take a moment to share a handful of nuggets regarding decision-making that may be helpful to you:

- Decide to always connect with what's real.
- Your time is precious. Don't waste it on what does not align with you and the more important people and things that need your attention.
- Decide to fully commit to being action-oriented and teachable.
- Avoid being indecisive.
- Refuse to stay in your weakness. Decide and strive to grow, to get better.
- Put your focus and energy into building the positive rather than worrying about eliminating the negative. Focus on growing the tree, not on killing the weeds!
- You and only you choose your actions.
- Greatness is achieved when you decide to take positive and productive action.
- Decide that you will not take shortcuts.

- Avoid paralysis by analysis. Refrain from overthinking. Don't talk yourself out of doing what may be advantageous for you.
- Implement a new idea or insight each day.

Life provides us with many illustrations of decision-making. Sailing is an intensive activity that mirrors decision-making at a microlevel. Reacting to changing conditions in sailing is like taking the process of decision-making and condensing it. Without the intensity, we fool ourselves into missing the big opportunity. Decision-making—combined with action—allows us to discover certainty. It turns uncertainty into certainty.

Life is a feedback loop—it's just that we are blind to it. We allow ourselves to believe decisions are binary—a simple yes or no. Underthinking and overconfidence are indicators that we've forgotten that life is a feedback loop. Life doesn't stand still—and neither should our decisions.

TAKE Action

> "Take time to deliberate, but when the time for action arrives, stop thinking and go ahead."
> **—Andrew Jackson**

Put on your seat belt, because what I'm going to share with you next will probably make you uncomfortable, scare you, motivate you, and transform you. My objective is to be ruthlessly honest with you by letting you know that absolutely nothing will happen if you do not take action. Talk is cheap; *walk* has meaning.

Here are my Dos and Don'ts on the topic of implementation.

DO	DON'T
• Strive to be proactive. The quicker you act on a decision made, the faster you will get results. • Focus on being disciplined and diligent. Order enhances careful and persistent work and effort. • The important actions are often the uncomfortable ones, so do what you need to do whether you like it or not. • Identify the critical few action steps needed to achieve your goals. • Create a well-thought-out plan and strategy to enhance focus, save time, and increase the probability of success. • Play to win. Don't be afraid of making mistakes. • Beware of distractions. Keep your eyes on the prize!	• Don't stay still. Nothing good comes from being in neutral. • Don't waste your time on things that are not important. • Your time is precious. Don't waste it on things that don't align with you and the more important people and things that need your attention. • Don't be an I'm-gonna-do-that-soon type of person. • Don't wait until the perfect day to act. The perfect day will never come. Today is the day! • Avoid overthinking. Paralysis by analysis cripples success.

There are three different types of people:
1. People that make things happen
2. People that watch things happen
3. People that say, "What the hell just happened?"

If you do nothing, you'll be the third type. That's a status I don't recommend for anyone. When in doubt, always ask, "What is the next right thing to do?"
- Taking action has fantastic benefits:
- Your self-esteem increases.
- Your confidence in yourself grows.

You feel better about yourself. You may not feel like taking action, but once you start, it always feels good. With every small step you take, you wow yourself.

Making a habit of taking action is priceless, because it fills you up, little by little. When you open a faucet slightly, the water drips slowly—but eventually, it fills the sink. When we take action, we get filled up with all that is positive. Remember, it's not about taking large steps; it's the small steps that lead to accomplishments.

> **James 2:26**
> *For as the body without the spirit is dead, so faith without works is dead also.*

Now that you are well-versed in what to do and what not to do, I recommend the following method of execution:
1. Visualize your outcome.
2. Imagine the steps to get there.
3. Take actual steps.
4. Check off the steps you've taken.

Celebrate your progress. Make action your goal! The actions you take, the steps you implement, are 100% in your control. Because of this, I strongly recommend that you become obsessed with the process, one that you create and implement. The very act of becoming an action-oriented person builds self-confidence and self-esteem. You will learn to enjoy the journey just as much or more than achieving the final goal. Along the way, you'll build character and backbone that will serve you when you encounter inevitable obstacles on your path. The idea of making action steps your goal, step by step, one small victory at a time, will lead you to the great accomplishments you've dreamed about. Your cherished goals await—all you need to do is take the first step.

Everything I've shared with you so far—from the cancer wake-up call to my self-discovery and the creation of my new life philosophy—would mean nothing if I never acted on it. I had to walk my talk. Chapters 5 and 6 are all about what I did: The plans I had and how I acted on them.

Key Points

- Taking charge of your life is the biggest responsibility you have.
- Never relinquish your leadership to another person, and never leave the fulfillment of your vision in the hands of others.
- Purpose is pursued, not programmed. It is a manual process, not an automatic process.

Ruthlessly Honest Questions

1. Do you live your life with a purposeful philosophy, or do you just go with the flow?

   _____
   _____
   _____

2. Are you aware that your life today is the result of your past choices?

   _____
   _____
   _____

3. Are you a person that waits for things to happen, or do you make things happen?

   _____
   _____
   _____

4. Do you have mental toughness?

   _____
   _____
   _____
   _____

> "Your life is not a rental; you own it."
>
> **—PETE DE LA TORRE**

PART III

Walk the Talk

CHAPTER 5
Wellness Trifecta

After many days of prayer, reflection, planning, and strategizing, it was time to step out into the world. God's instructions to me were crystal clear; now, it was game time. The whistle had blown, and I needed to kick off my rejuvenated life.

The question was, what was the first step? I had many options to consider: My health, my business, my family, and my community, among other things. They were all important, but one area was the top priority, without a shadow of doubt: My wellness.

Remember, the primary inspiration for my new life was my cancer ordeal. Our well-being is the foundation of everything. Let's take a closer look at what that means for us.

A Healthy Mindset

I spent over two months consumed by the troubling fact that I had joined the unwanted world of cancer. From the time of my biopsy to the day of my surgery, I suffered acute uncertainty and anxiety such as I had never felt before. These intense emotions forced me to withdraw from others. At times, I felt incredibly disconnected from the world. My fear isolated me. I was grateful for the reassurance from my loved ones that everything would be okay. However, when no one was around and I was by myself—especially when I went to bed—my mind was tempted to go into a dark place driven by fear.

During those moments, I had to strap on my seat belt, face the challenge, and decide to change how I was thinking. I decided to shift my attitude and embrace positive thinking. Instead of allowing myself to be sucked in by worst-case scenarios, I chose to focus my thoughts and energy on solutions, to spend more time on what could go *right* instead of what could go *wrong*. I convinced myself that I was going to beat cancer, and I did! I became a champion in the most important way possible.

As a result of that experience, I have been awakened to a new perspective, one that many times can only be attained through adversity. By the grace of God and my connection to him, I'm here today and able to share this story with you. My mind has been refreshed with a new outlook and an exciting sense of freedom. Anything is possible!

How many times have we heard the statement, "You become what you think about"? How do you feel when you hear this? Does it scare you or excite you? Do you feel an overwhelming sense of responsibility when it dawns on you that it's totally up to you to think about whatever you choose? Do you connect with what is positive or what is negative?

Being accountable for what we think about and understanding that we *choose* our thoughts is a powerful and awesome truth. Keep in mind that the quality of our lives is predicated on what we choose to think about and act on. Our thinking either makes us or breaks us. Your mind is either be your greatest friend or your worst enemy. What will you choose?

When my doctor told me, "You have prostate cancer," it felt like a bucket of ice was thrown at me. I could not connect with the news. I was in denial. Things like that usually happened to someone else, not me. The awful, scary word *cancer* can take over your mind in an instant, especially if it's your first time dealing with a health crisis, as was the case for me. My life flashed before me. I saw nothing but darkness and doom. Frank Sinatra's song "My Way"— which I happen to love—was in my head. I kept hearing the phrase, "The end is near, and now I face the final curtain." Not a good moment at all!

Eventually, I regained my composure, and reality set in. The intense fear subsided, and I was able to settle down and think more clearly. The threat of cancer or any other disease can affect your mind considerably.

How do we handle these threats? What do we do? What should we think about? Once the smoke clears, it's best to shift your mindset and begin considering the facts of the situation. In my case, I had a cancer diagnosis and I needed to find a way to be healed from this menace that was threatening my life.

Reality thinking—a way to think constructively and objectively based on facts rather than emotion—is critical upon hearing bad news. You have a problem, so now what? Denying the reality of a challenge is counterproductive; the more you sweep anything disagreeable under the rug, the more the dust of the situation builds up. Don't avoid unpleasantries. Sooner or later, you must do what is necessary, whether you like it or not. When my doctor broke the news to me, I was reminded of 2 Timothy 1:7.

> **2 Timothy 1:7**
> *For God hath not given us the spirit of fear; but of power, and of love, and of a sound mind.*

Consistently meditating on God's word provides us with a shield that will deflect negative thoughts of impending doom. The power of God is stronger than anything, and when you use his weapons to fight back against negative thoughts, you will win! Rest on him; he will get your mind right! However, you must do your part.

Start with an attitude of acceptance and a decision to roll up your sleeves and face the crisis with courage and resolve. That's half the battle. Yes, it is a battle to keep your mind focused on what may go right rather than what may go wrong. The human mind defaults to thinking about the worst that can happen. It takes determination and tenacity to think positive, productive thoughts. It is *simple*, but not *easy*. Yet it can and must be done!

Our well-being, powered by our mindset, must be our number-one priority. The mind is part of what I call the wellness trifecta, a harmonized combination of mind, body, and spirit. These three aspects of our person, working together and connecting with each other, create a powerful force that allows us to live our lives to the fullest. Our physical health is paramount. If we're not feeling well or we're dealing with a debilitating illness, it's extremely difficult to function and be productive. We may have trouble doing our work or enjoying time with family and friends. If our spirit is down, filled with doubt, sadness, or anxiety, we tend to live unhappy lives. However, in my opinion, the most important of the three (mind, body, and spirit) is our mindset. It is a certainty that our thinking is directly and powerfully interconnected to the quality of our lives.

With an optimistic and cheerful attitude, we can conquer the world.

> *"Whatever your mind can conceive and believe, it can achieve."*
> **—Napoleon Hill**

If you embrace and adopt this mindset, nothing can stop you from reaching your ultimate goals. There's just one caveat: We must choose to think positively, to think winning rather than defeated thoughts. When we face a challenge in any area of our lives, we have to focus on the solution and avoid dwelling on the negativity of the situation.

Without a doubt, the biggest challenge we can face is bad news regarding our health. The possibility of a terminal condition can destroy our spirit and our mindset.

Sooner or later, we all face health challenges. It's a piece of cake to think positive thoughts when you don't have a worry in the world. But we need to build our mental muscles, making our mind stronger and better suited to handle the next crisis. When the mind works overtime, we can expect sleepless nights. The good news is that the same energy that goes into negative thinking can be flipped to positive thinking. You have the power to shift your thinking. Allowing negative feelings to influence your mindset is fatal and can lead to a total disconnect from all that is good.

When you implement a winning attitude, determined to take life on instead of letting life take you through unexpected challenges and bad news, no person or situation can defeat you. Feed your mind with a vision of being a person that confronts misfortune with courage and fortitude.

Choose to be a solution-oriented thinker. Your well-being, which includes your body and spirit, is controlled by your mind and the thoughts you allow it to embrace. My mind was tested during my cancer ordeal. I thank God that I overcame that trial. I know more challenges will come my way, but now I'm stronger than I've ever been, especially in terms of my mindset. Our mindset is the catalyst for our well-being. Make sure your mind is connected to all that is good.

A Healthy Body

To be clear, I'm not a health expert. However, I have a body, just like you. We all can take care of and nourish our body with the right food, exercise, and rest. Unfortunately, millions of people treat their bodies harshly, without any idea what they're doing to themselves. Obesity is an epidemic, causing many people to develop multiple diseases and leading to early deaths. Our bodies are an example of connecting. Each organ has its function and is connected with the next one. We must make sure that these connections aren't unnecessarily clogged with toxic elements from eating the wrong foods. Who are we to abuse our bodies? We forget that God has gifted us with our body.

> **1 Corinthians 6:19-20**
> *What? know ye not that your body is the temple of the Holy Ghost which is in you, which ye have of God, and ye are not your own? For ye are bought with a price: therefore glorify God in your body, and in your spirit, which are God's.*

That's a huge responsibility. Why do we mistreat what God has given us free of charge? Why do we set up our bodies for failure? Why do we invite illnesses like cancer to invade our bodies?

I knew that, at some point in my life, I would be faced with a health challenge. I've been fortunate to enjoy relatively good health; I've seen many people pass through one sickness after another. When we're stricken with bad health, we typically go see our doctor to find out what's going on. Sometimes an illness is treated with medication; if it's something more serious, it may be treated through surgery. No matter what, the goal is to heal the malady and feel better.

Once we get back on our feet, what can we do to make sure we don't end up with another illness? How do we take care of our body so we can live free of unnecessary ailments? What can we do to feed our bodies with nutrients that prevent new diseases from invading us?

It's not that complicated. If we eat the right foods, take our vitamins and supplements, and exercise, we should be fine. Sounds easy—but it takes a bit more than just talking about it: We have to *do* something about it. Doing something about it requires sustained discipline and commitment to our health. It is imperative that we reconnect our bodies with healthy foods that connect us to a healthier lifestyle.

Why is it that adversity is needed before we make long-contemplated changes in our lives? Why does an illness like cancer wake us up and force us to take action? The fear of death is a great motivator. When we're threatened with death, our perspective changes dramatically, and we become willing to do whatever we have to do. The problem is that we enjoy being comfortable. Some people are just plain lazy, living carefree lives and hoping they can go through life without lifting a finger. If we want something bad enough, we'll make it a priority and get it done. There is no other way. If our most precious commodity—our health—is threatened, we'd better adopt the mindset to get in shape. Living a healthy life requires seeing our doctor and getting an annual physical. The best time to do this is at the beginning of the year when your motivation is at its highest, driven by your New Year's resolutions. God willing, all will be good, and you can move on about your business.

My encounter with cancer kicked me in the butt. It was a wake-up call on steroids. In the aftermath of my surgery, I decided to make the wholesale changes that were needed in order for me to feel, look, and live better. I am convinced that the stress we encounter each day is frequently the root cause of our illnesses. Simply put, the process looks like this:

STRESS > DIS-EASE > ILLNESS

When I was diagnosed with cancer, I suddenly became obsessed with taking care of my body by eating the right foods, exercising, getting plenty of rest, and letting go of stress. I was going to be a new man, making my health my top priority. I learned that eating the right foods is not so much about avoiding or fighting disease; it's about building a foundation that allows us to feel good physically and that enhances our self-esteem. Once you are physically fit, your body will be your shield, fighting off potential diseases trying to sneak up on you. Through my cancer battle, I learned that if you take care of your body, your body will take care of you.

A Healthy Spirit

There are some defining and significant events that have a dramatic impact on our lives. Some of them are positive, and some are not. Either way, we're changed forever. In my case, I had cancer; by the grace of God and a successful surgery, I am cancer-free. A troubling occasion became a blessing in disguise; it opened my eyes to see that what I thought was unattainable is actually possible. I have a sense of freedom I had never experienced before, and

I'm more convinced than ever that (1) there is a God and (2) I'm not him (thank God!). I don't have to try to understand everything in life—the pressure is off.

> **Proverbs 3:5-6**
> *Trust in the Lord with all thine heart; and lean not unto thine own understanding. In all thy ways acknowledge him, and he shall direct thy paths.*

Prior to my diagnosis, I believed in God and trusted in his work and blessings, but I had never really been tested. Facing an illness that I might not survive was the ultimate challenge. I had no choice but to trust the Lord to get me through that unwanted situation. I could have responded with a why-me or this-sucks attitude. I could've been swallowed up in self-pity. But I felt I had no right or reason to complain. Any attempt to discern why I had cancer and why now would have been a waste of my time; it also would have burdened my loved ones and close friends with my whining. I believe that God has been, is, and will always be in charge. He knows what he's doing. Who am I to question him?

The spirit is the third part of the wellness trifecta. Spirit means different things to different people. For me, it's the experience of an unseen, hard-to-explain state of being that brings in peace, harmony, and well-being. I don't question it; I don't try to label it. I trust it and have faith that it's protecting me from all that can harm me. It leads me to do what is right and guides me toward the right places and people. This Spirit, which I call God, is my Savior. His presence invigorates my soul with unparalleled energy and passion. Whatever wisdom or discernment I have is a direct result of my relationship and deep connection with him and my abiding by his word.

Trusting in a power greater than yourself is liberating and powerful; it causes you to know deep down in your core that all will be taken care of. When we develop a relationship with God, we know that all is and will continue to be well, despite any challenge that may come—including a bout with cancer.

As I look back on my life, I see that God has been there every step of the way. I've lost count of the challenges (some self-induced) that he's pulled me through. He has never abandoned me or let me down. I'm reminded of the famous poem, "Footprints," which says, "During your times of trial and suffering, when you see only one set of footprints, it was then that I carried you." The good Lord has carried me through more personal hiccups than I can even remember.

Regardless of whatever difficult times I have had or will face in the future, I know he is with me. Whenever I feel powerless, I plug in and connect with the greatest power in the universe: The one and only God!

Many people try to play God. They use their God-given intellect to try to figure things out. These are also those who are constantly worrying about one thing or another. In my twenties, I went through a rough patch emotionally, experiencing intense anxiety and fear. I went to speak with a priest about what I was going through. As I was sharing my situation with him, he told me something that has stayed with me ever since. He said, "When you pray, why worry? If you worry, why pray?" Think about that for a moment. We either trust God or we don't; it's that simple.

The word *good* equals God! All the goodness in the world is 100% influenced by the Spirit of God. Every kind act and the love we share with others is a direct result of his presence. The nonnegotiable core values we hold dear are clearly instilled in us by him. We honor him by striving to always do the right thing, working hard, and serving others. Living the good life is not about the riches we enjoy, our material possessions, or the luxury lifestyle we may be blessed with; it's about living a life of integrity and authenticity. Experiencing abundance is not about money and possessions; it's about tapping into the never-ending resources that God has supplied us with. If we truly believe in his goodness, we will enjoy the fruits of his blessings— even things that may appear at first to be disastrous. Remember this the next time you pass through a dark tunnel in your life. Connect with God, and the light will appear.

Key Points

- Our well-being, powered by our mindset, must be our number-one priority.
- If you take care of your body, your body will take care of you.
- Trusting a power greater than yourself is liberating and powerful; it causes you to know deep down in your core that all will be taken care of.

Ruthlessly Honest Questions

1. What do you think about most of the time?

   _____
   _____
   _____

2. Do you believe that stress and bad eating habits can cause disease, or is sickness just the result of bad luck?

   _____
   _____
   _____

3. Do you ever doubt the power of God?
   _____
   _____
   _____

4. Do you embrace and live by the wellness trifecta?
   _____
   _____
   _____
   _____

"The sweetest harmony is a sound mind, a healthy body, and an inspired spirit"

—PETE DE LA TORRE

CHAPTER 6

Business Transformation

A New "Why"—A Repurposed Business

The adversity I experienced over a two-year span in 2020 and 2021 from Covid-19 and my cancer ordeal forced me to reevaluate my life, including my business. I was compelled to ask myself tough, honest questions:

- Why am I in business?
- What is it that I do?
- How should I do it?
- Who is my business for?
- Where and when am I carrying it out?

After an intense personal evaluation, I decided to reinvent and restart my business, which I had launched ten years earlier. Before I began recreating my business plan, I paused and asked God, my number-one business advisor, for guidance and inspiration.

> **Proverbs 16:3**
> Commit thy works unto the LORD, and thy thoughts shall be established.

When you create a business plan and share it with God, he can make sure that you accomplish it. Invite God to be part of your business every single day for it you do, He can propel you for on-going sustainable success. If you do, you will encounter a new and profound faith in your business.

Before I recreated my business plan, I needed to understand that my success was predicated on utilizing my God-given talents; I needed to find out what I loved to do. All of us have special talents, and I'm no exception. But our talents are not a guarantee of success. They have to be cultivated; otherwise, they'll go unused, and God's gifts will be squandered. He intends that our talent enrich the world and enrich our lives. Value the gift God has given you; nourish it, make it grow, and share it with the world.

> **1 Peter 4:10**
> As every man hath received the gift, even so minister the same one to another, as good stewards of the manifold grace of God.

The idea of reengineering my business reinvigorated my entrepreneurial spirit. I had newfound enthusiasm, energy, and creativity, new ideas and insights. The sky was the limit, because God had whispered in my ear, "Go for it. I have your back!" I had an intangible business tool—the wisdom that's only acquired by overcoming adversity and learning from the experience.

As I retooled my business plan, I was reminded that a business is driven by its vision, mission, and core values. Before any enterprise is launched, the organization's "why" must be clear to all. You need to know without a shadow of a doubt why your business exists. Your ideas and offerings must fully align with each other. As you prepare your business plan—and before you launch your endeavor—it is paramount that you understand what you plan to do for your clients and why. The way you serve the market will loudly speak forth your core values—the things that are most important to you. If a business exists simply to make money, it will die an early death. But if the reason you have a business is to make a positive difference in the lives of your clients, you are on the right track. I was given the green light to start all over again with a new perspective and a repurposed vision, mission, and core values.

> **Vision**: A spirited and productive connection with key executives and entrepreneurs who multiply business opportunities and create strategic win-wing partnerships and business synergies.
>
> **Mission**: To be an "implementation catalyst," inspiring and connecting business professionals for long-term and sustainable business growth.
>
> **Core Values**: Knowledge, Excellence, Leadership, Integrity (K.E.L.I.).

Most businesses and corporations proudly showcase their vision, mission, and core values. The question is, how many of them *practice* what they preach? Are their vision, mission, and core values authentically connected? In most cases, they do not connect. Most business owners quickly forget why they're in business in the first place. They operate their companies with a mindset to sell, sell, sell, no matter what.

The real purpose of any organization is to serve the needs of the customer, to serve the customer's well-being. No matter what your service or product is, it's important to do business with integrity, transparency, and the highest ethics. Before you hit the streets with your offering, make sure you're not taking any shortcuts. Always serve your clients by doing what is right.

Remember that doing business is never a one-way street. Your business should offer a win–win for all involved. It is imperative that you communicate this message clearly with your market.

Covid-19 and cancer opened my eyes to what is most important in my life, including why and how I run my business. As an entrepreneur, it's in my DNA to be creative and resourceful. God has blessed me with me with courage and determination, despite many roadblocks. It is incumbent on me to apply my God-given talents and experiences for the benefit of my clients. That means I need to set an example of doing what is right and delivering on the value I promise to them. After all, God—the greatest CEO ever—always delivers on his promises to us. I'd be very proud to write a resounding five-star review on the Yelp of life thanking God for his outstanding service to me!

Cancer and Covid-19 revolutionized my life and my business. They both happened within the same twelve-month period. I believe the two are connected. Without cancer and Covid-19, we may have never connected. This book and the ideas I'm sharing with you are a testament to my transformation. I awoke to a new life and a new business model. My brand, Pete Connects, was inspired by this life experience. I have a repurposed business that, for the first time ever, aligns perfectly with the way God has always wanted it to be.

Win, Win: Make a Difference

It is impossible to separate a personal challenge from the business you run, especially if you are an entrepreneur. What happens to you personally crosses over into your business, the products and services you offer, and how you deliver them to your clients. Your business and personal life are undeniably connected.

Overcoming a difficulty builds character and gives new meaning to your life. You acquire a fresh outlook that allows you and your company to thrive. Why does this happen? It's simple—it's because you are doing what is right for your clients. You are looked upon as a legitimate problem-solver, a solution-driven professional. You operate your business with integrity and a win–win attitude. It is obvious to everyone that your intentions are good. You haven't fallen into the trap of being money-hungry; rather, you're someone who clearly wants what is best for his clients. Instead of having to push for business, you attract clients. An I-am-not-desperate-for- business motto is 100% more appealing to potential clients, because most people don't like to be sold to; most people prefer to decide for themselves if they want to purchase a product or use your services. Your business becomes magnetic; potential clients gravitate to you. You don't need to promote your offering to them. The big picture—all that you do—is transformed.

What was important to you in the past isn't that important anymore. By the same token, what was formerly not important is now a front-and-center priority. Everything you do has a more profound meaning than ever before.

Prior to my surgery, I ran my business with the mindset of hustling and making money. Although I had significant experience, knowledge, talent, and connections, I never realized my full potential. I never made significant money, even though I tried hard. I was always on the go and in survival mode. I did business with just about anyone that would pay me. This approach held me back significantly. I played and thought small. A lot of my efforts were on things that would pay my bills but wouldn't necessarily fulfill me. Without realizing it, I fell into a rut. When things were going well, everything was great. However, when I experienced a slump, my self-esteem hit rock bottom. My identity was directly tied to the money I had in the bank. I cheated myself and my clients for years by not producing my best. I misused my time on activities that didn't connect well with myself or the clients I was chasing. I failed to realize that God created me to do specific work that would not only showcase my unique, God-given talent but would also serve the market with much better results.

One result of my cancer experience was that I reexamined what I was doing in my business and how I was carrying it out. I dissected my business, especially the value I offered and delivered. I had cut corners in the past, but that way of doing business wouldn't work anymore—I wouldn't be able to live with myself. When God save me from cancer, he gave me a second chance, an excuse to restart my business as if I was launching it for the very first time. The detailed work of the medical team—the way they led me through the surgical process—impressed me so much that I was compelled to emulate their professionalism and apply it to my business.

I restructured my processes with new and reinvigorated purpose. I became very honest with myself, realizing that I didn't have all the answers and that it was okay to seek help. I sought the opinions, advice, and mentoring of successful business leaders. I no longer had to know everything. I enjoy and appreciate expert advice from the right people. The bottom line for me was clear: Do things the right way and for the right reasons. I didn't have to reinvent the wheel; I just needed to implement what I had learned for the benefit of my clients.

When cancer shook me up, a significant thing happened: I rediscovered who I am and the purpose God has for my life. This applied particularly to how I ran my business.

> **Ephesians 2:10**
> For we are his workmanship, created in Christ Jesus unto good works, which God hath before ordained that we should walk in them.

The good Lord created me in a very special way to do his work. I had a competitive advantage over everyone in my field—there was no other Pete De La Torre in the world. Once I internalized this fact, I was empowered beyond description. I had a new sense of freedom. I could run my business the way I wanted to, serving like-minded, spiritual people with similar core values. I had a unique set of skills that no one else could offer. This realization reminded me of a line from the movie *Taken*: "I have a very particular set of skills, skills I have acquired over a very long career." God gifted me with unmatched uniqueness.

Now, the question was, how was I going to use my skills? My value proposition had to personify my uniqueness as a person and as a professional with a particular set of skills. God blessed me with creativity, the ability to take a blank canvas and create something new. I could use that creativity in my business. I was given the green light to create something new that could make a significant difference in the marketplace. I no longer had to run my business with my energies focused on my competitors.

The stage was set, and I was ready to move forward with my new, reinvented business. The question was, how would I get the word out? How would I acquire new clients? It was crucial that I get my message out effectively, so that everyone would know what I did and how I could help them.

I took a deep dive into how I could better market my services. I initiated a new routine in which I visualized switching hats and pretending I was the prospect. I discovered that there's no better way to understand and serve your clients than to put yourself in their shoes. I needed to let them know that I was just like them and that I could be trusted. In my marketing, I needed to connect authentically and with integrity. I revamped my existing platforms, including my award-winning talk show, social media sites, newsletters, blogs, articles, and website, using simple, plain language that expressed precisely what I wanted to say and connected with potential clients. With the help of marketing experts, I was able to create a unique look and feel that would attract the right prospects, clients who would gain the greatest benefits from my services.

Once you acquire new clients, you must provide exquisite service. Your work as a problem-solver—the main reason they hired you—must be delivered as promised and in a timely manner.

In addition, I had something more I wanted to offer my clients. Being reborn after my cancer struggle, living each day in gratitude to God, the medical team, and my family and friends, motivated me to go one step farther in everything I did, including my business. I want to enhance each client's experience by showcasing their business and opening doors for them to connect with the right contacts and opportunities. I want them to look good and feel good about themselves and their business. My spirit was ignited in my recovery, and I wanted to pass the fire on to my business and clients. How could I make their lives better? How could I inspire them to achieve their own greatness, their own prosperity? I hope my business will indeed be a difference maker in the lives of my clients, their families, and the community at large. **Pete Connects was born.**

Giving Back—Corporate Responsibility

> *"We make a living by what we get, but we make a life by what we give."*
> **—Winston Churchill**

As business owners or professionals, we serve our clients by being problem solvers and opportunity finders, and we earn income for the work we do. We do our job as promised; therefore, all is well. However, if we are to have a long-term, sustainable, and rewarding business, we cannot underestimate the enormous benefit of giving back not only to our clients but also to the communities that are home to our businesses. The value I provided to my clients had to go a step farther. Most of the people in my community were not my clients, but they needed to benefit from the presence of my business. If I was to be a true servant, everyone within reach of my business, either in person or virtually, needed my help and support.

In order to fulfill the calling lovingly placed on my by the Holy Spirit, I needed to be the embodiment of providing value across the board, beyond my direct business activities. God blessed me with success in my business. It was my obligation to pass that blessing on to others, to share my good fortune. When I looked at all the people I had connected with, I realized the enormous responsibility I had. I was an influential person, a connector. I've been in leadership roles for most of my life, and I had a platform for communication and connecting that very few have—my long-running talk show. Finding paying clients is necessary and important, but I needed to offer far more through my business. I needed to give back to others whether they were clients or not. The marketplace had rewarded me with monetary success; now, I had to return the favor by connecting with and giving back to my community.

For businesses that are selfish, hoarding their success, the clock is ticking. Sooner or later, their success will dwindle; it's not sustainable. The more we give to others, the more we give to ourselves. Giving back should be in our DNA. By the grace of God, I am here today and in good health. He provided me with an opportunity to refresh my business with a new outlook to serve and give back, especially to those in great need. When I support those who are less fortunate, I provide them with an opportunity to achieve their dreams.

I was clear that I had to partner and connect with my community. Every company bears a corporate responsibility to make a positive difference by supporting local causes, including charitable organizations. Every company should serve and give back to those in great need. Community grows out of the sense of responsibility we have toward each other. In the Bible, God encourages us to take care of our neighbors—whether they are friends or enemies! We must remember the importance of maintaining connections with each other and focusing on building a community of love through words and actions.

When we hear about economic development, we typically think of job creation and the growth of local businesses. Our business transactions have a direct or indirect economic impact in our community. But giving back is more than the money we give; it's also the information and inspiration we provide. I have been blessed to host an award-winning talk show for the last twelve years. My content and dynamic guests have made a significant and positive impact in the lives of thousands of people in the US and around the world. All of it is free to my viewers and listeners. It's my way of giving back without any expectation of return. In fact, my content and the topics we discuss have taken on new meaning because of my battle with cancer. God's Spirit and guidance comforted me through this scary and eye-opening moment in my life.

> **2 Corinthians 1:4**
> Who comforteth us in all our tribulation, that we may be able to comfort them which are in any trouble, by the comfort wherewith we ourselves are comforted of God.

My task is to use my voice, inspired by God, to comfort others and connect them to newfound hope.

In addition to being a catalyst of hope, I also seek to be a messenger of wellness. In Chapter 5, we focused on the wellness trifecta of mind, body, and spirit. We are placed in this world to live the healthiest life possible by thinking the right thoughts, eating the right foods, and feeding our spirit with all that is good. We all have a calling to be a person that spreads the word and leads by example, promoting wellness in our relationships, health, and businesses. Our business will thrive on all levels because of what we do for our clients and our philanthropic efforts.

Remember, we are leaders in the business world and in the communities we serve. People look up to us, whether we realize it or not. Our role is to set an example. Businesses have a unique opportunity to make a significant difference in the lives of their clients and the communities they serve. Being a community partner is good business.

Key Points

- When you create a business plan and share it with God, he can make sure that you accomplish it.
- It is impossible to separate a personal challenge from the business you run.

- As business owners and professionals, we serve our clients by being their problem solvers and opportunity finders.

Ruthlessly Honest Questions

1. How much of you is in your business?
   _____
   _____
   _____
   _____

2. Are your business activities well-connected and aligned with your vision, mission, and core values?
   _____
   _____
   _____
   _____

3. Do you practice corporate responsibility, or do you just give it lip service?
   _____
   _____
   _____
   _____

4. When asked, what do your clients say about you?
   _____
   _____
   _____
   _____

"When given the opportunity, choose to transform your business"

—PETE DE LA TORRE

PART IV

The Road Ahead

CHAPTER 7

Dig Deep, Rise Above, Reach Out, and Stay the Course

Your Call to Action

You have taken time out of your busy life to read up to this point. What are your thoughts about what you have read? How do you feel? Are you inspired? Have you learned anything? Do you relate to my story? Do my words resonate with you?

As I mentioned in the introduction, my intent in this book was to share an experience in my life that shifted my foundation dramatically, a moment that redirected the course of my life. Before my cancer ordeal, I was getting ready to write my first book. I was going to share my life story and how I came to be the person I am today. However, my prostate cancer intervened, an unprecedented challenge in my life. Stuff like this always happened to someone else. I was very fortunate that it hadn't happened to me yet.

> "Adversity is always unexpected and unwelcomed. It is an intruder and a thief. But in the hands of God, adversity becomes the means through which HIS Supernatural Power is demonstrated."
> —Charles F. Stanley

We all know that, sooner or later, we'll face a health challenge or some other adversity, one of those things that always seems to happen to someone else. Such challenges shake us to our core. We are never quite ready to handle this kind of disruption in our lives. It seems that we are tested unfairly, without being given time to study and prepare. Things just happen! The question is, what now? What are we supposed to do? How do we deal with these kinds of things?

As you read the introduction and the subsequent chapters, you found out how I dealt with my cancer experience. I had no choice but to pass through that trial, step by step. I was blessed by the guidance of God, the support of friends and family, and the expert hands of my surgeon, which put me on the path of healing for my body, mind, and spirit. At the time of my diagnosis, I didn't realize that this unwelcome health crisis was the best thing that ever happened to me. My body was healed, yes—but I learned lessons and gained wisdom that bolstered my life in a way that would never have occurred without the challenge I faced. Everything has changed! I was gifted with a new beginning, a new life.

My family life is better than ever, my connection with close friends has new meaning, my business has been revitalized, and I have become wiser. But most importantly, my relationship and connection with God is stronger and deeper than it has ever been. I want the same for you. My desire is that you would make positive and meaningful changes because of my story. Let's discover how you can be blessed as well.

At this very moment, you may be going through some sort of adversity—perhaps a health challenge, a financial setback, or a family crisis. If you aren't, I can guarantee that at some point down the road, you will. How you respond to sudden adversity is a testament to your character and will undoubtedly shape your life forever. Your response determines your next steps, positive or negative. You have an opportunity to make a difference in your home, your workplace, and your community. Share the truth. Inspire others with powerful insights you have discovered on your path, insights that can create long-lasting transformation for them as well.

Your Path

> **Persian Maxim**
> *"And this too shall pass."*

Wherever you may be at this very moment in your life, this too shall pass. Both good and bad times come and go; they never stay for long. This season in your life may be happy or sad. If you're in a moment of happiness, you hope it'll stick around indefinitely, and if you're in a tunnel of darkness, you hope and pray that it'll end soon. Your life to this day has been an interesting journey, to say the least. You've experienced joy and sadness, success and failure, achievements and disappointments. Wherever you may be on your path, you have come from somewhere, and you are going somewhere. The long and winding road of your trip has been a combination of smooth travels and bumpy terrain. Allow me to be ruthlessly honest—this will continue for the rest of your life. As I mentioned previously, your life today is a byproduct of your thinking and choices. Before you, there is a golden opportunity to alter your life's path and the quality of your life. So, what will you choose?

The following are hard-nosed questions I have for you. They are designed with tough love and are intended to push buttons within you that motivate you to take positive and decisive action:

1. Challenges will come, sooner or later. How will you respond? What will you do?
2. What do you do when adversity knocks on your door? How have you handled trials in the past? Did you learn anything? What have you done with what you've learned?
3. Are you grateful for the people in your life, your family and friends? What do they mean to you? Are you there for them when they need you? How will you help others through their trials? Are you spending quality time with your family and friends?
4. Do you believe in a power greater than yourself? Has God saved you—gotten you through previous challenges?
5. Professionally, why do you do what you do? Are you running your business for the right reasons?
6. Has a personal challenge—one you've overcome—changed your business in any way?
7. Have you learned from adversity?
8. Are you really living your life, or are you just getting by?
9. If you're sleepwalking through life, what will wake you up? Do you need adversity to wake you up—a challenge, a health scare? What alarm will reach you? How close does an emergency need to be to move you to action or shake you up?
10. Do you have the endurance to go through life without taking shortcuts?

The Freedom to Succeed

If you want to be successful in personal and business life, you need to be free. Freedom means:
- Being ruthlessly honest in every aspect of your life
- Thinking and doing what is right and honorable
- Taking the high road despite distractions and deceit
- Disconnecting from people and situations that are misleading and dishonest
- Avoiding, at all costs, short-term gratifications that surreptitiously incarcerate you

If you're ready to live a full and free life, please heed my advice and consider the following four things as action items for the rest of your life:

1. Dig Deep

Your greatest opportunities are the ones that lie deep within you, like hidden treasures. These opportunities are the key to a life worth living. But many times, we don't know that they are hiding within us. We look elsewhere to find these treasures. The following is a short story that illustrates this idea.

Russell Conwell, the founder of Temple University, gave a speech titled "Acres of Diamonds." He told a supposedly true story about an African farmer named Ali Hafed who heard stories of fortunes found by other farmers. They discovered diamonds on their land and became rich beyond their wildest imagination. Ali Hafed grew discontented with his life and desperately desired the same kind of fortune. He sold his farm, left his family, and began a quest for riches. He searched through many lands, far and wide. As an old man, he became depressed and despondent. He threw himself into a great tidal wave and was never seen again.

The successor to his land, another farmer, strolled one day along a creek that ran through the property. He noticed a blue flash in the creek bed. He knelt and sifted through the water until he pulled a crystal object from the mud at the bottom of the creek. He wiped it off, took it home, left it on the mantel above the fireplace, and quickly forgot about it.

Several weeks later, a visitor stopped by the farmer's house and noticed the crystal on the mantle. He picked it up and became excited—he was holding a diamond in his hand. The farmer protested at first, but the visitor reassured him that it was, indeed, a diamond. That farm eventually became one of the largest diamond mines in the world. Had Ali Hafed known how to look for and identify diamonds, he would have had the fortune he so desperately wanted.

The lesson of this story is simple: You don't need to look elsewhere for opportunity, achievement, or fortune. All the opportunities you need can be found right where you are now. You are standing among acres of diamonds.

When you take the time to dig deep within yourself, you will be amazed at the diamonds you will uncover. Going within yourself can be a beautiful experience filled with insights and discoveries that are astonishing, that will blow you away. Yet let me caution you, as you dig deeper, you will encounter resistance. Old relics like limiting beliefs that can block your path. You will need courage and persistence to continue digging, yet you must not stop. The further you go, the more you will find out how truly unique and special you are.

You must always look at the big picture and look at it as often as you can on any given day. This practice is best described as meditation and reflection. A special and quiet time to disengage from the world around you, to connect with yourself but most importantly to the Spirit of God. His presence, which is always with you, can be your guiding light. Tapping into his power provides you with wisdom and perspective. All this is possible if you let it happen.

Embarking on this internal voyage and doing it regularly will give you the freedom to be creative, to discover your true purpose and connect with what is most important to you. You will honestly know what it is you must pursue and how to do it. You will learn to love yourself and others as you tap into your heart more and more. Remember, if you desire to grow as a person, you must do it from the inside out. Your time alone with yourself and God is yours, something that no one can take away from you.

2. Rise Above

Imagine yourself riding in a helicopter with an unmatched vantage point. You can look down at what's below you, but at the same time, you can also see to the horizon. You see what's happening now, but you can simultaneously take a sneak peek at what's waiting in the distance.

I recommend that you take the findings of your personal gold rush, the hidden treasures you've discovered during your reflection time, and rise above to look at the big picture of your life.

Rise boldly as far as you can, thrusting yourself above the clouds of pessimism and doubt to carry your message of hope and empowerment to others. Keep in mind that there is no top floor in life. Keep taking steps upward to the next floor.

When you're flying high, inspired by the Spirit of God, you become a force for good. You set an example of being a better person in all areas of your life by treating others with respect and dignity. The right people will gravitate to you because of your ruthless honesty and authenticity. Your decision to fly above the dark clouds will inspire others to do likewise. Make sure to think, speak, and act like a winner. When you keep looking up, anything is possible. Rise above!!

3. Reach Out

Once you discover your golden nuggets it's time to spread the wealth and proactively reach out to others. Your family, the business world, and community need you. It's imperative that you pass on what God has freely given to you. If you hoard your newfound treasures, you'll stifle your growth and end up back in a life of emptiness.

> **The Prayer of St. Francis:**
> *Lord, make me an instrument of Thy peace. Where there is hatred, let me sow love.*
>
> *Where there is injury, pardon. Where there is doubt, faith.*
>
> *Where there is despair, hope. Where there is darkness, light. Where there is sadness, joy. O Divine Master,*
>
> *Grant that I may not so much seek to be consoled as to console, To be understood, as to understand;*
>
> *To be loved as to love.*
>
> *For it is in giving that we receive;*
>
> *It is in pardoning that we are pardoned;*
>
> *And it is in dying that we are born to eternal life.*

My second chance at life and the wisdom I acquired meant that I had a duty to perform God's work on his behalf and leave a positive legacy for others to follow. It also meant that I needed to get out of myself to think about and serve others.

You bless yourself by blessing others. You gain by seeking to support others, particularly during their times of adversity. A self-centered person serves no one, not even himself. Get out of yourself and strive to be a beacon of light for someone else.

As you extend a helping hand, be careful not to make the mistake of enabling others. Seek to support others, but remember that you aren't responsible for their actions.

Just as you are accountable to do the right things in life, so are those you support. If they abuse your generosity in time and support and disrespect your intentions, be ruthlessly honest with yourself and them by letting them go. You must respect and honor your values without exception.

Apply all your energy to being a champion for goodness and wellness. Share your story with the right people at the right time and in the right place with the goal of converting adversity into victory. Be one of God's master connectors. Use social media technology to touch as many people as possible, in the right way and with the right message. Be an ambassador for gratitude. When we are grateful, when we acknowledge the goodness in our lives, we feel positive emotions, relish good experiences, improve our health, and deal with adversity so that we can build strong relationships. Never forget that you have a responsibility to represent God in all your ways. You've been designated a leader in your family, business, or community.

4. Stay the Course

You've probably heard the saying, "Life is a marathon, not a sprint." Life is a long-term experience, lived one day at a time—not a week or a month at a time. In fact, we live our life hour by hour, moment by moment. Live in the present, not in the past or the future. Live in this hour, this minute.

How are you living your life? Are you replaying the past, obsessing over past mistakes? Are you projecting into the future, bringing on unnecessary and unreasonable anxiety? If so, you're not enjoying the gift of today. Don't live with one foot in the past and one foot in the future. Worry about tomorrow when tomorrow arrives, not today. Each day has enough trouble of its own.

Don't worry about things that haven't happened yet. Live in the moment, and leave your worries for tomorrow. One of the greatest truths we can ever learn is that life is difficult. Once we accept this reality, we can move forward with the freedom to live it fully, one moment at a time, without anxiety for may go wrong down the road.

The road that lies ahead is unknown. No one can predict what we'll encounter, what great dreams we'll achieve or what adversity we'll have to face. Only God knows. He knows because he has already designed our entire life, from start to finish. If you're reading this book having survived previous challenges, then you still have unfinished business that needs your attention. From this moment on until the good Lord tells you it's over, get to work fulfilling his purpose for you. He has further plans for you, and he expects you to be at your best as you complete the mission.

With this in mind, knowing that you are responsible, I urge you to implement the following course of action:

- ASAP: Always Stop and Pray. Connect with God constantly.

- Make the wellness trifecta a priority.
- Say "I love you" to your family members at least once a day.
- Take one bold step each day.
- Dream big dreams.
- Live your life with ruthless honesty.
- Be grateful for every day.
- Look for the good.
- Seek to understand and help others.

My friend, none of us knows what the future holds. The road ahead is uncertain and sure to be filled with both smooth and treacherous stretches. We'll achieve great things and meet stressful challenges. We don't know how long we'll live; it may be many years or, God forbid, we may be gone sooner than we expect. There is no point of arrival; we keep going until it's our time. God is calling the shots, and he decides when it's over.

My final message to you is this: Each day when you get up in the morning, with all the energy you can muster, thank God for another day, a day that brings the possibility of extraordinary connections, unprecedented opportunities, and uncommon success! As each new day arrives, make it count!

God bless you.

Key Points

- Wherever you may be at this juncture in your life: This too shall pass. Both good and bad times come and go; they never stay for long.
- Your greatest opportunities are the ones that lie deep within you.
- Keep in mind that there is no top floor in life. Make sure to keep taking steps upward to the next floor.

- Apply all your energy to being a champion for goodness and wellness, to sharing your story with the right people, at the right time, and in the right place with the goal of converting adversities into victory.
- From this moment until the good Lord tells you it's over, get to work fulfilling his purpose for you.

Ruthlessly Honest Questions

1. Is there any idea or insight shared in this book that you will apply today?

   _____
   _____
   _____

2. Do you believe that you can make a positive difference in the world today?

   _____
   _____
   _____

3. Are you willing to share your personal story?

   _____
   _____
   _____

4. Is being "at your best" really that important to you?

   _____
   _____
   _____

"A house or a building is not built by its design; it is built by a commitment to build it"

—PETE DE LA TORRE

ACKNOWLEDGMENTS

First and foremost, I want to thank God, who was my writing partner. The words in this book were inspired by his love and grace.

I thank my wife, Jacquelyn, for her unwavering love, support, and inspiration. She believed in this project ever since we reconnected over two years ago. When I first shared the idea of writing my first book, her words to me were simple: "Do it!" I had been thinking and talking about writing a book for over thirteen years. I had the intention, but I procrastinated, waiting for the perfect time to start. Connecting with Jacquelyn after all these years became that perfect time.

My younger brother (lovingly known as Dr. Phil) wrote and published his first book, *How Leaders Keep the Fire*, in 2021. His determination and grit inspired me to finally move forward with my book. While still working on his book, he took the time to kick me in the butt and get me going—that is, to start writing. His enthusiasm for my book topped my excitement. That, my friends, is an example of selfless love!

I probably would not be here today and most definitely would have never written this book if not for my urologist and surgeon, Dr. Jason Wolf. His straightforwardness about my cancer and his expertise saved my life. I owe him an eternal debt of gratitude. I salute you, Dr. Wolf!

When I started my book project shortly after my surgery, I was headed down the path of self- publishing my work. Along the way, I ran across two old friends of mine, authors Cheli Grace (Book to Millions®) and Manuel Torres (Book to Legacy®). They are the founders and principals of Delian Origin Publishers. Their expertise, methodology, and knowledge guided me through the book-writing process. This finished product is a direct result of their commitment and professionalism. Thank you very much!

I am grateful to the following for their partnership and support:

- John and Carlos Gazitua, Sergio's Restaurant, Miami, FL.
- Juan Del Busto, Del Busto Capital Partners, Miami, FL.
- Juan Manuel Fayel, Antonio Franco, and Carolina Otero, JMF Consulting, Doral, FL.
- Adriana Parra Simon and Rosalyn Long, Candlewood Suites, Miami Intl. Airport, 36 Street, Miami, FL.
- Monica and Luis Llerena, CBT College, Miami, FL.

ABOUT THE AUTHOR

P**ete De La Torre CSSYB**, is an award-winning talk show host, motivational speaker, productivity expert and business development specialist. With over 40 years of hands-on experience in 5 different industry sectors, he is considered one of the most influential business and thought leaders impacting the lives of millions worldwide.

Pete has served The South Florida and Global Market in different capacities. representing key sectors such as: International Business, Economic Development, Financial Services, Corporate Training and Media. His key objective and purpose are to teach and inspire his clients to experience significant success in their business while enhancing their lives.

Community involvement has been very important and he has held key positions with several non- profit and business organizations in South Florida which include the following groups: Miami Children's Hospital Foundation, American Heart Association, A Safe Haven for Newborns, Suniland Optimist, The International MBA Advisory Board of Florida International University, The Greater Miami Chamber of Commerce, Chamber South and an Executive Board Member with The Coral Gables Chamber of Commerce.

Among his recent awards and recognitions, his talk show is proud to be the recipient of "The 2015 & 2016 SBA Small Business Media Advocate of the year" for South Florida and The State of Florida. This award is given by The Small Business Administration "SBA", a nationwide government entity geared to promote and support small business all over the United States.

He attended Miami-Dade College and Florida International University in Miami, Florida. He is a graduate of the Hispanic Leadership Academy at The University of Chicago Booth Business School and has a Lean Six Sigma (Performance Improvement Method) Yellow Belt Certification.

RESOURCES

I highly recommend that you take the time to read these outstanding books. They have impacted my life profoundly, and I believe they will inspire you as well:

- The Holy Bible, New King James Version, Copyright 1982
- 100 Days of Trusting for Men, Family Christian Stores, Copyright 2009
- Perfectly Yourself, Discovering God's Dream for You, Matthew Kelly, Copyright 2006 and 2017
- The Magic of Thinking Big, David J. Schwartz. PH.D., Copyright 1959,1965
- Secrets of The World Class, Steve Siebold, Copyright 2009 Simple Truths, LLC
- Just Shut Up and Do It, Brian Tracy, Copyright 2016 Simple Truths
- The 12 Week Year, Brian P. Moran and Michael Lennington, Copyright 2013
- How Leaders Keep the Fire Lit, Phil De La Torre, PH.D., Copyright 2021
- Blue Ocean Strategy, W. Chan Kim and Renee Mauborgne. Copyright 2015
- The Roadless Traveled, M. Scott Peck, M.D., Copyright 1978

MOVING FORWARD WITH PETE

Watch and listen to "Pete Connects" Podcast:
www.petedlt.com/#podcast

Get inspired as "Pete Speaks":
www.petedlt.com/#speaker

Learn at "Pete Connects U":
www.petedlt.com/#training

FOLLOW AND CONNECT WITH PETE

Website: www.peteconnects.com Email: Pete@peteconnects.com

YouTube Channel: Pete De La Torre

Linkedin: @Pete De La Torre Facebook: @PeteDLT

Instagram: @PeteDLT

Made in United States
Orlando, FL
06 May 2024